THE RELUCTANT EVANGELIST

By the same author:

KNOWING GOD'S WILL

The Reluctant Evangelist

PAUL MILLER

KINGSWAY PUBLICATIONS
EASTBOURNE

Copyright © Paul Miller 1990

First published 1990

All rights reserved.
No part of this publication may be reproduced or
transmitted in any form or by any means, electronic
or mechanical, including photocopy, recording, or any
information storage and retrieval system, without
permission in writing from the publisher.

Biblical quotations are from the
New International Version © 1973, 1978, 1984 by the
International Bible Society.

Front cover illustration by Taffy Davies

British Library Cataloguing in Publication Data

Miller, Paul
The reluctant evangelist.
1. Christian church. Evangelism
I. Title
269'.2

ISBN 0-86065-796-5

Printed in Great Britain for
KINGSWAY PUBLICATIONS LTD
1 St Anne's Road, Eastbourne, E Sussex BN21 3UN by
Courier International Ltd, Tiptree, Essex
Typeset by Nuprint Ltd, Harpenden, Herts AL5 4SE.

Contents

Foreword

Most Christians who take the Bible seriously would agree that evangelism—that is, sharing our faith with other people—is important, but many of us have the mistaken idea that it is a job best left to experts.

Even the most cursory glance at the New Testament reveals that, for the first Christians, faith-sharing was not an activity exclusively confined to church leaders. We read of ordinary men and women gossiping the gospel in normal, everyday situations. Michael Green makes the point in his contemporary Christian classic *Evangelism in the Early Church* (Hodder; reprinted by Highland) that 'the little man, the unknown ordinary man who left no literary remains, was the prime agent in Mission' (page 208).

In many parts of today's world, the church is growing at a remarkable rate. When you get to the stories behind the statistics, one interesting factor emerges: the church is growing fastest through ordinary Christians sharing their faith in daily living.

A few years ago, I attended a conference of Christian leaders in Latin America. Talking with a pastor from a country that is witnessing rapid church growth, I asked him for some insights into what was happening. He told me of the way in which new Christians are trained and encouraged to be witnesses for Christ from the moment of their conversion. Everyone was taught the 'why' and the 'how' of evangelism. In his country, he told me, it was the *people*, not just the *pastors*, who took evangelism seriously.

It seems to me that we need a radical dose of this same medicine if we are to see the continent of Europe, and other Westernised nations, reached for Christ. But where do we begin? Some of us feel reluctant, tongue-tied or plain embarrassed when it comes to talking to someone else about our faith in Jesus Christ. We live with the fear of losing our friends or appearing fanatical if we get too excited about our beliefs.

This is a helpful book for those who want to do something to overcome their natural reluctance about evangelism.

I have enjoyed reading Paul Miller's book for three reasons.

First, because it is a book written out of personal experience. Paul Miller writes from what he has seen and done. Because of this he avoids high-minded theories about evangelism and provides an honest and readable guide for those who want to learn how to share their faith effectively.

Secondly, this is a book rooted in Scripture yet refreshingly related to today's world. To be both biblical and relevant is a goal to which every Christian communicator should aspire.

Thirdly, this is an immensely practical book geared to action rather than armchair philosophy.

Paul Miller is an enthusiast and his enthusiasm is infectious. You may not agree with everything he says but I am sure, like me, you will find yourself stirred to prayer—and action!

It was said of the early Christians that 'those who had been scattered preached the word wherever they went' (Acts 8:4). As we move into the last decade of the twentieth century, it is my prayer that we will see another generation of Christians equally committed to influence their world for Christ.

IAN COFFEY
Field Director
Evangelical Alliance of Great Britain

Preface

I became a missionary without even knowing it. After my conversion to Christ while in India in 1972, I was making my way overland back to Europe, stopping at Christian ministries on the way. The very first name on my list was one Floyd McClung in Kabul, Afghanistan.

After our initial meeting I was invited over for tea, stayed the night, stayed the month, and then just stayed. Nearly twenty years later and I am still with Youth With A Mission. I came for tea and stayed a lifetime. God pulled a fast one on me!

Never in my wildest dreams had I imagined myself as a missionary or an evangelist. But God, who is as committed today to Mt 28:19 ('Therefore go and make disciples of all nations') as he was when Jesus first said it 2,000 years ago, was determined to see his work accomplished even through the likes of me. He called me— and when that was not sufficient he pushed and shoved me.

A bit of push and shove was necessary as I was that

typical biblical figure: the reluctant hero. God has ever had two sorts of servants in his camp: lion-hearted, great souls eager for action; and faltering, reluctant heroes. The lion hearts are the Davids—David's only response upon being confronted by that nine-foot mountain Goliath was a cool, 'Who is this uncircumcised Philistine that he should defy the armies of the living God?' (or, 'Who the heck does he think he is, this oversized oaf?' 1 Sam 17:26). They are also the Pauls—in the teeth of a rioting city, Paul wanted to stand up and address the assembled throng (excellent opportunity to preach! 'Now that we are all here together I wonder if you could just turn in your Bibles to...') only to be dissuaded by the wiser counsels of his anxious and concerned friends (see Acts 19:30–31).

The reluctant heroes are the Moses—Moses who did everything possible to slink from under God's burden and call, who finally in a moment of inspired weaseliness presented God with his crowning thought (paraphrased), 'Here am I, Lord, send him!' (see Exodus 3:4, 11)—the timid Timothies, the Gideons. Where David was prowling about looking for giants to overthrow, Gideon was skulking about in caves, intent on avoiding conflict at all costs, content simply to survive, so panicked that he was threshing wheat in a winepress (Judges 6:11). Where David was perfectly happy to contend with Goliath in broad daylight before two watching armies, Gideon could only with a superhuman effort steel himself to cut down a few powerless idols in the dead of night (Judges 6:27).

Gideon is to David and heroism what Peter Sellers' Inspector Clouseau is to James Bond and spying.

But the point is that God gets his work done through both types. God worked on the Gideons and the Moses until they could stand tall and stand up for him. In obedience they learned valour. In the end their deeds were no less glorious than those of the lion hearts. Initially reluctant, they ended up heroes. 'They that know their God shall be strong and do exploits,' Daniel says.

If you feel like a reluctant evangelist then you are in good company. Don't despair of being used by God. The God of Gideon is your God too. God who persisted with Moses will persist with you if you, as Moses, will finally say, 'Not my will but yours be done.'

I too have been a reluctant evangelist. I have been a Saul hiding amongst the baggage until God, who has grown used to this sort of behaviour, graciously pulled me up by the scruff of the neck and set me on the road to walk with him as he reaches out to save his world. This book attempts to chronicle where God has taken me in evangelism and the lessons he has taught me on the way.

In my sixteen years with Youth With A Mission in Afghanistan, Holland and England I have been in a wide variety of evangelistic situations. It is out of these experiences that this book has grown. Lessons learned, mistakes made, accomplishments eked out—it's all in here. Anything which might be useful to you and which would make me look as good as possible... I have thrown in unstintingly!

PAUL MILLER

I

The Significance of the Insignificant

I was hot, tired and in India. More specifically, I was in
Mussoorie, a lovely town set in the foothills of the Hima-
layas. Trudging wearily up one of Mussoorie's steep
roads looking for a place to sleep I saw an elderly Indian
gentleman cross the road and come towards me. As he
was about to pass me by he startled me by reaching out
and gripping my arm. He then amiably asked me what I,
an obvious foreigner, was doing in his fair country. My
reply that I had been there for the past six months to
seek peace through yoga and meditation was all that he
needed. He eagerly launched into a brief explanation of
his own Christian beliefs and why I should adopt them. I
had just been evangelised!

Such a simple step—cross the street and talk—but
what a momentous one. To some, at that moment, he
might have seemed a busy-body sticking his nose in
where it did not belong; to others he might have seemed
a do-gooder benignly wasting his time and mine; but to
me, old Mr Hiram was the messenger of life. In the

15

course of the following week, the earnest convictions and practices of years were overturned. I became a Christian. I, who had once scorned Christians as weak and narrow-minded, now joined their ranks to follow the resurrected Galilean. Years of emptiness were brought to an end. God became a reality. New challenges, new joys, new difficulties and a new direction in life were now mine.

I felt a little like the early disciples must have felt when their humdrum lives were turned topsy-turvy because they had come into contact with the Messiah. Before they met Jesus everything had been so simple; they had been born fishermen and they would die fishermen. But then Jesus came and before they could snap their fingers and say, 'Pontius Pilate,' they found that they were the pillars of a worldwide organisation called the church which was soon to change completely the whole of the Roman Empire. Already this church was, in the words of some, 'turning the world upside down' (see Acts 17:6). Certainly my world had been turned upside down, my life revolutionised because someone had pointed me to Jesus.

Is evangelism important? The real question is: Is anything else important? Jesus knew what he was talking about when he said, 'What is highly valued among men is detestable in God's sight' (Lk 16:15). Note the contrast: upon winning the World Cup the streets of the lucky South American capital may explode with all night celebrations, but scarcely a heart skips a beat in heaven. And consider: the response among my mystical, Eastern companions to my conversion account was studied indifference or a polite, if uncomprehending, 'How nice,' whereas in heaven it was party time. Jesus gave us a fascinating glimpse into the goings-on in heaven when he said, 'There is rejoicing in the presence of the angels of

God over one sinner who repents' (Lk 15:10). South American football mania had nothing on that scene. One cannot imagine the rejoicing of angels being a tame affair. There is nothing tame about these creatures who, far from being butterballs on wings, were such majestic beings that they overawed John—who really knew better—into worshipping them (Rev 19:10; 22:8).

The simple conversion of a single person causes all this commotion. The angels are thrilled about evangelism. God gets excited about evangelism. Yes, evangelism is important.

Jesus said of John the Baptist that 'among those born of women there is no-one greater than John' (Lk 7:28). John, that first-century hippy, greater than Alexander the Great, Julius Caesar and the other giants of world history? John greater than Moses, who was 'more humble than anyone else on the face of the earth' (Num 12:3) to whom 'the Lord would speak . . . face to face, as a man speaks with his friend' (Exod 33:11)?

What made John greater? To the high and mighty he would have been a 'nobody' with a 'nobody position' from a 'nobody country'. Luke might well have been deliberately contrasting Pilate head of Judea and Herod head of Galilee with John head of nothing (see Luke 3:1–2). Yet Jesus said he was the greatest on the earth. His greatness was not to be found in his dazzling personality, stylish camelhair overcoat, nor even in his sterling character (many other biblical heroes were his equal in devotion, sacrifice and spirituality). John's greatness was to be found in this one act: he introduced Jesus to the world. 'The reason I came baptising with water was that he might be revealed to Israel' (Jn 1:31). He was simply an usher. All the prophets prophesied about Jesus, but John was unique in that he actually ushered in the real person of Jesus: 'But what did you go out to see? A prophet? Yes, I tell you, and more than a prophet. This is the one about whom it is written: "I will send my messenger ahead of you, who will prepare your way before you" ' (Lk 7:26–27).

John was special because he rolled out the red carpet for Jesus which the King then stepped down upon as he broke into world history. And this is what all evangelism is: rolling out the red carpet so that people might meet the King.

Evangelism is God's dynamite. Evangelism transforms individuals' and people's eternity. But the gospel not only fits man for heaven, it equips him for earth. It changes not only individuals but whole cultures. Modern, secular, Western culture may not want to acknowledge its debt to the gospel, but that debt remains. The West would have little of what it now enjoys and takes for granted had it not been for the transforming power of the gospel. The gospel through the centuries shaped values, honed expectations and quietened fears. It made science possible and opened the way for political and economic development. (See Appendix.)

Evangelism is not a grubby little activity on the sideshow of history, fit only for quacks and hair brained enthusiasts. No, it is central to time and eternity. 'It is the power of God', the dynamite of God to transform individuals and whole cultures. No wonder Paul said, 'I am not ashamed of the gospel' (Rom 1:16).

The significance of the insignificant

On the surface, the simple business of telling people about Jesus, someone who, after all, lived on this earth all of 2,000 years ago, hardly seems so significant. Isn't story-telling something one can leave for the leisure hours after the real work of the day is done? Can an evangelist's practical importance really be compared with a nation-leading Prime Minister's, an opinion-moulding newspaper editor's, or a live-saving doctor's?

Surely this is why Jesus gave us the parable of the mustard seed: 'The kingdom of heaven is like a mustard seed, which a man took and planted in his field. Though it is the smallest of all your seeds, yet when it grows, it is the largest of the garden plants and becomes a tree, so that the birds of the air come and perch in its branches' (Mt 13:31–32).

Jesus is getting across two basic points here: first, that the mustard seed seems so totally insignificant, so small and weak. Can twelve Galilean 'hicks'[1] along with their carpenter leader really change the world? They had no army and no wealth. They sought not the domination of nations but the liberation of individuals. They sought service, not glory. The obvious first question about such a gospel would not have been whether it could influence our world but whether it even had a hope of survival in a dog-eat-dog world. Behold the mustard seed, the small-est and most insignificant of seeds.

Jesus' second point was that this seed might start as the tiniest seed yet it would grow to be the largest and most impressive plant in the entire garden. Here Jesus was only echoing the Old Testament theme given to Daniel:

In the time of those kings, the God of heaven will set up a kingdom that will never be destroyed, nor will it be left to another people. It will crush all those kingdoms and bring them to an end, but it will itself endure for ever. This is the meaning of the vision of the rock cut out of a mountain (Dan 2:44–45).

The rock in Daniel's vision seemed so much less

impressive than the 'enormous, dazzling statue, awesome in appearance' (Dan 2:31), but it eventually became the greatest. It spread through the whole world. And it spread because people spread the seed of God's word. This kingdom, starting so small, overtook temporal kingdoms and lasted for ever and ever and ever; and for ever is a long time! That which seemed the most insignificant turned out to be the most significant.

This is evangelism: the significance of the insignificant. Evangelism is talking to people about Jesus. Can this really be a force for revolutionising the world for good? Can we really hope to make a dent in the huge problems our world faces simply by talking to people one by one? The *Mustard Seed Conspiracy* says yes.

Consider this story that Tom Sine relates:

His rough, gnarled hands gently scooped dirt over the seed as the sun warmed the good earth. He walked several more steps, thrust his shepherd's staff into the ground, and planted another seed. Every day he spent all his daylight hours walking the barren hillsides of Provence planting seeds while his sheep grazed.

In 1913 the Provence region in southern France was a desolate area, denuded of trees because of overcutting and overintensive agriculture. Most of the wildlife was gone, water holes had dried up, and most of the inhabitants had given up on the area, too. But not the old shepherd. Every evening in his small cottage he sorted acorns, hazelnuts, and chestnuts for tomorrow's planting.

One day a young man happened on the shepherd and asked, "What in the world are you doing, anyway?" "Well, it is pretty obvious what I am doing: I'm planting trees." "But it will be years before these trees will do any good!" "Yes, but some day they'll do somebody some good, and they'll help restore this dry land. I may never see it, but perhaps my children will."

Twenty years later the hiker returned to Provence. He

was amazed to find the old shepherd still alive and still sorting nuts in his cottage. But he was even more amazed to see the countryside. The entire valley was covered with a beautiful natural forest of all kinds of trees. Life had returned to the barren valley. Wildlife had returned, and the farmers had come back to cultivate the soil again.

A delegation of the Chamber of Deputies from Paris came down to see the miraculous forest. They saw the entire region of Provence restored—its wildlife, agriculture, and population. And they honoured the man who brought the valley to life again.[2]

Can the seemingly insignificant be significant? Can twelve loaves really feed five thousand? Yes, in God's hands. That's the story of the gospel. But first we have to make our loaves available. We have to get involved. And that's the story of our next chapter.

2

Here Am I, Lord, Send Him

We are not all evangelists, but we are all witnesses. Evangelism is a spiritual gift only given to some (Eph 4:11), whereas witnessing is a role for all.

In investigating a crime, when the police ask all witnesses to please come forward, they are not looking for clever people who have an outstanding gift in expressing themselves. They are not looking for talent; they simply want somebody who was on the scene of the crime and can tell them what they saw or heard. Witnessing is simply telling what we have seen and heard (Acts 22:15). The very fact that we are Christians means we have seen and heard something of Christ which we can give witness to. All Christians can do this.

Peter Wagner differentiates between Christian roles which we all have and spiritual gifts which only some have. He writes,

> . . . some have the gift of ministry or serving (Rom 12:7), but all Christians should serve one another (see Gal 5:13). Some

have the gift of exhortation (Rom 12:8), but all have a general role of exhorting one another (see Heb 10;25). A few have the gift of evangelist, but all Christians are expected to exercise their role of witness (see Acts 1:8).[3]

The practical implications of what he is saying are threefold. First, we should not feel guilty if we are not constantly winning people to the Lord. Evangelism is a gift which we may not have. Secondly, we should structure our main ministry and time around the gifts we have, not the gifts we do not have. Again, we should not feel guilty if we are not spending all our time evangelising. Thirdly, we should not use 'non-giftedness' as an excuse for completely neglecting our Christian roles. All of us, as Christians, need to fulfil our role as witnesses even if we do not have the gift of evangelism. In fact, you will probably never discover whether you are gifted in evangelism until you open your mouth and begin to witness.

If we neglect our role as witnesses, the gospel will not spread as God intends. The gospel first broke out among the Gentiles of Antioch not because the big-time evangelists (Philip, Paul, etc) held a campaign there, but because ordinary Christian witnesses 'gossiped' the gospel to their neighbours. The result? 'A great number of people believed' (Acts 11:21).

Joseph Aldrich tells the legend recounting the return of Jesus to glory after his time on earth.

Even in heaven he bore the marks of his earthly pilgrimage with its cruel cross and shameful death. The angel Gabriel approached him and said, "Master, you must have suffered terribly for men down there."

"I did," he said.

"And," continued Gabriel, "do they know all about how you loved them and what you did for them?"

"Oh, no," said Jesus, "not yet. Right now only a handful of people in Palestine know."

Gabriel was perplexed. "Then what have you done," he asked, "to let everyone know about your love for them?"

Jesus said, "I've asked Peter, James, John and a few more friends to tell everyone about me. Those who are told will in turn tell other people about me, and my story will be spread to the farthest reaches of the globe. Ultimately, all of mankind will have heard about my life and what I have done."

Gabriel frowned and looked rather sceptical. He knew well what poor stuff men were made of. "Yes," he said, "but what if Peter and James and John grow weary? What if the people who come after them forget? What if way down in the twentieth century, people just don't tell others about you? Haven't you made any other plans?"

And Jesus answered, "I haven't made any other plans. I'm counting on them."[4]

Jesus is counting on us. The very picture the Holy Spirit has given us of the 'body of Christ' (Eph 1:23) makes this clear. God is our director and energiser, but we are his hands and his feet and his mouth. Where we go, he goes. Where we do not go, he, by and large, does not go.

If I had been God I think I would have done it all rather differently. Rather than counting on twelve fallible men I would have extended Jesus' lifetime to match Moses'. After all, in 120 years you can do a lot of good. Having completed his three-year assignment in Judea, I would have then sent him on to Samaria and then on to the uttermost parts doing three-year stints in each nation. In this way he could have covered thirty nations by the time he was 120 years old. Think of the impact. Imagine Jesus in China!

Moving down the centuries a little, let's try a different approach there too. Rather than counting on lots of ordinary Christians to spread this message throughout the earth, had I been God, I would have raised up 223 super-evangelists, one for each of the nations. 'A Billy Graham for Every Nation!' Splendid. Just sprinkle them liberally around the world, add a dash of anointing and, hey presto, the job is done.

But God, in his wisdom, went a completely different route. Why? First, because he makes way for all manner of giftings, the great and the small, the apostle Pauls who win nations and the Ananiases who only win one (but what a one!). Each one is necessary and important. God is not besotted with superstars. 'God chose the foolish things of the world to shame the wise' (1 Cor 1:27).

Secondly, God chose this route because his method is multiplication, not addition. Would you rather have one million pounds a day for five weeks or one pence doubled every day for five weeks? The first is much more attractive at first glance. Addition of big sums rather than multiplication of small sums always look more impressive. But here's what your increase looks like as you go along:

	Adding millions	Multiplying pence
Day 1	£1,000,000	1p
Day 2	£2,000,000	2p
Day 10	£10,000,000	£5.12
Day 20	£20,000,000	£5,242.88 (the month is almost up and you're still way behind. But now watch.)
Day 31	£31,000,000	£10,737,417.24
Day 32	£32,000,000	£21,474,835.48
Day 35	£35,000,000	£171,798,688.00 (pence lazily rounded off!)

Maybe God's ways are better after all! The world can

be reached much more effectively by each individual Christian reaching their neighbour, who reaches their neighbour, who reaches their neighbour and so on, than it can by bringing in the big guns every ten years for one big campaign.

God's plan is to involve everyone in evangelism. Without our involvement it remains just that, a plan and nothing more. With our involvement God's plan becomes reality.

Involvement, however, because it calls for risk, effort and sacrifice, is often the last thing in the world that we want. We can easily empathise with Moses who, hearing God's call for involvement, remembered Aaron and heroically said, 'Here am I, Lord, send him' (see Exodus 4:10–17). As if there were not enough obstacles in the way of us getting involved in God's great plan, we Christians have added a few more for good measure: the 'involvement blockers'.

Involvement blockers

'I don't believe in talking. I believe in being. It's not what you say but who you are. We need to live Christianity, not talk Christianity. The witness of our lives is the most powerful tool we have.'

'I believe in spontaneous evangelism, not in planned evangelism. See how spontaneous was Jesus' evangelism. He did not have planned campaigns. He evangelised the people as he met them in the course of the day.'

'I believe in "come and see" evangelism (see John 1:39). The early church did not have to use door-to-door campaigns, but were so filled with the Spirit of God and so living as the community of the redeemed that people

27

were attracted. They could come and see the reality of God rather than just hear about it.'

Do any of these sound familiar? They are common enough Christian convictions which, if seriously held to, will hinder the church embracing biblical evangelism. This sort of thinking will keep us quiet and prevent us from taking initiative in evangelism. And if the church does not take the initiative in evangelism who will? I doubt if the Devil will and we cannot expect the unbelievers to. Let's take these objections one at a time.

'I believe in being more than talking'

But talking is crucial to evangelism. There is no evangelism without some communication of God's word. Even great miracles do not constitute evangelism. At Pentecost, it was the miracles which won attention, but preaching which won converts—'When the people heard this, they were cut to the heart' (Acts 2:37). Miracles say, 'Here's God,' but we still need the preacher to say, 'And here's what God wants.' Evangelism starts with seeing God at work and ends with understanding God's mind.

It was not ultimately the apostles' works that the priests feared but rather their words—'They were greatly disturbed because the apostles were teaching the people and proclaiming in Jesus the resurrection of the dead' (Acts 4:2). Not only did they fear it, but their preaching was the one thing the priests actually forbade: 'But to stop this thing spreading any further among the people, we must warn these men to speak no longer.' (Acts 4:17). It was not the miracles they objected to, but to the apostles' interpretation of the miracles. The apostles could do as many miracles as they wanted, just so long as they didn't preach Jesus.

Speaking the message was one thing the apostles were

resolutely determined not to give up: 'Day after day, in the temple courts and from house to house, they never stopped teaching and proclaiming the good news that Jesus is the Christ' (Acts 5:42).

The priests knew and the apostles knew and Jesus knew that the gospel message was powerful. They knew ideas have power. Jesus talked about 'the key of knowledge' (Lk 11:52, NASB). Knowledge of the gospel is a key opening the door to a relationship with God. But knowledge that is not communicated does little good. My knowledge of hygiene does not help the mother in Afghanistan whose children are dying from the dirty water she gives them. She needs this knowledge herself; someone needs to communicate it to her. That is why talk is important.

Jesus believed in talking. Fifty per cent of his ministry was talking (Acts 1:1). Jesus was talking constantly: 'Every day I was with you, teaching...' (Mk 14:49). For Jesus, compassion sometimes was expressed in doing, in giving concrete assistance (Mt 20:34) and sometimes it meant talking: 'When Jesus landed and saw a large crowd, he had compassion on them.... So he began teaching them many things' (Mk 6:34). This is hardly the activity of one who views words as of little importance.

'I believe in Jesus' style of spontaneous, not planned, evangelism'

But Jesus' style was planned evangelism. How did he come to earth in the first place? He wasn't just strolling through heaven when, tripping over a harp carelessly discarded by an angel off on some cosmic mission, he stumbled and fell down to earth; at which point he thought he might as well make the best of a bad situation and, now that he was down here anyway, do something about the sorry state of the world. Not likely! Jesus 'was chosen before the creation of the world' (1 Pet 1:20) to be the Redeemer. His way was well prepared with prophecies about his work, his companions, his betrayer, his sufferings. It was all minutely thought through.

The redemption of the world was not something that was just going to happen spontaneously. God deliberated and set out on a course of action. Jesus went through with it not because he had a spontaneous personality but because he 'resolutely set out for Jerusalem' (Lk 9:51). He followed his predetermined course of action rather than following his present whims.

This is not to say, of course, that there is no place for the spontaneous. Jesus was spontaneous within the confines of a general plan. He made plans as to where he would travel, and then as he met people along the way he would take opportunities to share God's word. But even these occasions for spontaneous evangelism owed a debt to planning. If he had not followed his plan but rather just waited at home for opportunities to present themselves spontaneously, 98% of the gospels would never have been written.

The apostolic method was an interplay between the planned and the spontaneous. The explosive growth of the Gentile church in Antioch (see Acts 11) was the result of spontaneous witnessing, but note that the Antiochan Church did not set this approach in concrete as *the* way to church growth. It was from the Antiochan Church that the first great planned, thought through, purposeful effort was made to reach the 'uttermost parts'. Paul did not just 'happen' to find himself wandering through Asia Minor; he was sent out with a specific mission by the Antiochan Church. And so the gospel spread.

If we ran our entire church programmes on the same spontaneous lines we run our evangelism programmes we would be in trouble. Can you imagine it: 'Fellowship groups and congregational worship will take place this week as the Lord leads. We will just trust the Lord for it to happen and when it does we trust that there will be several of you in the same place at the same time as worship is difficult without worshippers. God bless and see you next week…maybe.' No, if we can plan worship, the intimate meeting of our spirits with God's, then we can plan evangelism.

'I believe in "come and see" evangelism versus the raiding party approach'

It is true that Jesus said, 'Come and…see' (Jn 1:39), but he also said, 'Go and tell.' That's what the Great Commission is all about. Central to the Great Commission is the little word 'go'. In fact, 'go' seems to be one of God's favourite words. He told Abraham to 'go'. He told the disciples to 'go'. He told his own Son to 'go'. If Jesus had practised 'come and see' evangelism in heaven he would have been waiting a very, very long time.

Many have reacted against superficial evangelism which is only concerned about giving words rather than giving ourselves. Our emphasis is consequently much more on quality relationships. Quality relationships take time. Quality relationships include shared interests not circumscribed by the one question, 'Are you saved, brother?'

But Jesus was not only concerned with building relationships, he was also concerned with communicating the word of God to as many people as possible. Breadth was as vital as depth. (Evangelists tend to think in terms of breadth where pastors think more exclusively in terms of depth. Thinking about the 75% fallout rate of Jesus' sower parable in Matthew 13, the evangelist, unperturbed, says a sticking rate of 25% of 1,000 converts is

31

better than 75% of 100 converts.) Jesus was willing to accept transitory relationships in his life if it meant he could reach more people with God's good news. We read in Luke 4:42–43 that 'the people...tried to keep him from leaving them. But he said, "I must preach the good news of the kingdom of God to the other towns also, because that is why I was sent." '

I think many of us today, had we somebody like this on our ministry teams, would have automatically corrected him. We would have counselled him and helped him to see that a less superficial, short-term approach was needed. We need to recover a belief in the power of the simple, unadorned word of God and then to go and tell it to the people.

You will have noted that among the weapons of our warfare listed in Ephesians 6 are gospel shoes (see verse 15). Now shoes are important for standing, but even more important for walking. Shoes enable us to 'go'. A warrior may look very impressive all decked out in his shiny armour and plumed helmet. He may momentarily slow down his enemy by making menacing noises and fiercely brandishing his sword. But if he continues simply to stand still and wave his flashy sword in the air; if he does not 'go' to where the enemy is; if he simply stays put and does not get within fighting distance of his enemy (you cannot sword fight at one hundred paces) then his enemy soon learns to disregard him as a mere windbag and gets on with his own destructive work. We are not a threat to the Enemy till we go to where the fight is.

Going and taking the gospel is part of our spiritual warfare which will free this earth from the dominion of Satan and bring in the kingdom of God. Paul, in writing Ephesians 6:15, was probably recollecting Isaiah 52:7 where the prophet says, 'How beautiful on the mountains are the feet of those who bring good news, who proclaim peace, who bring good tidings, who proclaim salvation, who say to Zion, "Your God reigns!" ' Feet must be one of the least attractive bits of the human anatomy, and yet the inspired writer calls them beautiful. They are beautiful because they are the key to getting this key message out to those who need to hear it. News has to be communicated to do any good to the man on the other end.

A newspaper carried a story of a Japanese soldier discovered in the deep jungles of the Philippines where he had been hiding and staying out of human contact for all of twenty years. He thought that World War Two was still on! Why? Because no one had told him otherwise.

Evangelism is about telling people that the war is over. 'We have peace with God' (Rom 5:1). How we can go about telling people this good news more effectively will be the subject of our next chapter.

3

Bold—More than a Soap Powder

'I don't think I ever met a Christian until I was twenty-five and, if I did, they certainly never blew their cover,' says John Wimber.

Overcoming the fear barrier is absolutely necessary to evangelism. Without boldness we will never 'blow our covers' and let people know we are Christians.

Without boldness there can be no evangelism. Christian wimps will never get the job done. That's why the early church made boldness a matter for specific prayer. In Acts 4:29 they cried out to God saying, '...enable your servants to speak your word with great boldness.' It took boldness to speak God's word 2,000 years ago and it takes boldness to speak his word today.

The early church not only prayed for boldness, they were characterised by boldness. It was the apostles' boldness which identified them in the Jewish priests' minds as 'Jesus people'. We read, 'When they saw the courage of Peter and John and realised that they were unschooled, ordinary men, they were astonished and they took note that these men had been with Jesus' (Acts 4:13).

At this point it was not the piety or the doctrine of the apostles which caught the attention of the priests, it was their boldness. The priests were not accustomed to theologically untrained yobbos speaking back to them with such conviction and confidence. The word for 'ordinary' is the Greek equivalent for our English word 'layman'. Laymen weren't supposed to speak so knowledgeably about God! Whenever they did speak about God the priests would airily dismiss it with, 'This mob... knows nothing of the law,' or 'How dare you lecture us!' (see John 7:49; 9:34).

In fact, the Greek word for 'ordinary' or 'layman' used here in verse 13 is the word *idiotes*; the root for our English word 'idiot'! And here these *idiotes* were speaking with such boldness. I can almost hear these thunderstruck priests thinking, 'All this seems vaguely familiar. Where have I seen such boldness before? I know, that Jesus fellow. This is that motley pack that always followed at his heels.'

The New American Standard Bible puts it like this: '...and began to recognize them as having been with Jesus.' The process is emphasised here—'they began'. There was a sense of a dawning realisation. Red lights were beginning to flash in previously complacent brains. Alarm bells were going like the clappers as the identity of these men began to dawn on them. But a much bigger and more momentous truth also came crashing in on them. Their thinking must have gone like this, 'Wait a minute, something awful is going on here. We thought we had finished all this off when we killed that spellbinding carpenter. But now there's twelve more just like him! It's not over; it's only just *begun!*'

We need boldness because, in doing evangelism, God

challenges us to go beyond our natural abilities and natural inclinations. There are times when he asks us to do things which rub against the grain; things we would never do unless told to do so by our Commander-in-Chief. We may not be in the habit of speaking to strangers—as a matter of fact I teach my children not to—and yet be called upon to do just this in order to share the love of Jesus. We may be shy and withdrawn and yet be called upon to reach out beyond our little, safe world and tell others what God has done for us.

It was in Nottingham during the winter of 1976 that I saw my first live street preacher. Theatrically waving his arms high over his head as he scowled and bawled out John 3:16 to an audience of none, the man was not my idea of attractive evangelism. I said as much to my wife as we hurriedly scampered past. She turned to me with a twinkle in her eye saying, 'Maybe you'll be doing that some day.'

'Fat chance,' I said, dismissing this bad joke.

I forgot all about it until God began to put an increasing burden on my heart to reach out with the gospel to the people of Nottingham. Paul's words became more and more meaningful to me: 'I have become all things to all men so that by all possible means I might save some' (1 Cor 9:22). Paul was not stuck on any particular means, he was stuck on the end of winning people to Christ. I, however, seemed to be stuck on the means of 'natural evangelism'. I found this stand-up-in-the-street-and-shout-your-fool-head-off approach unnecessarily obtrusive; bad form altogether. But God did not appear overly impressed with my arguments or taste preferences. Was my taste better than God's?

In the midst of my struggles with all this I went to church one Sunday and heard a man relating how, as a youth, he used to enjoy greatly his church's weekly Saturday outing. They would play football, then gather as a group on the green in front of the pub to sing, finishing off with someone standing up to give their Christian testimony. On one afternoon his usual joy and enthusiasm completely deserted him, the simple reason being that the group leader had informed him that today was his day to tell his story of what Christ meant to him. Dazed, he stood up, faced the pub and could only think to say, 'Jesus loves you.' His mind blank, he repeated it again a second time. And the third time was not dissimilar. Then, in total defeat, he sat down.

Nine months later, when this young man was telling this story in a neighbouring church, a man came up to him saying, 'I was in that pub that day and I would like to tell you what happened. Half drunk, I staggered out of there, and all I could hear as I shuffled down a back alley were these words echoing over and over again in my mind, 'God loves you. God loves you. God loves you.' From that moment I couldn't put the thought out of my mind. I began to seek God and here I am today a Christian.'

Upon hearing this story, I thought that if God could use the feeble efforts of this young man in the open air then he could use *my* feeble efforts in the open air. I didn't really care now whether this method was attractive, but whether it was effective.

So a friend of mine, one John Goodfellow, and I decided to go down to central Nottingham to try our hand at this novel approach. However, when we reached our chosen spot in the cold light of day we became acutely aware of a host of previously undiscerned and eminently sound reasons as to why our course of action should be deferred. Not altogether cancelled, mind you, simply put back til the 'fulness of time' should be divinely revealed. Like ranks of little soldiers, these arguments trooped past, file by file: it was too cold; or maybe it was too hot? On this particular day shoppers didn't seem to be in the mood for being interrupted by ranters, and being sensitive to the public was obviously a most Christian virtue, etc. This manifest common-sense had nearly persuaded us to call it a day when my wife (you husbands know what is going to come next, don't you?) said, 'No, I really think it's right that we are here. God has spoken to us.'

Grudgingly, we admitted she was right. But what should we say and how should we begin? I dreaded that first moment when startled pedestrians would look up at me in surprise thinking, 'Who is this nutcase bellowing to the treetops about God? Religious mania, obviously.' At that point I needed a good dose of Proverbs 29:25: 'Fear of man will prove to be a snare.'

The only way to escape a snare is to bust out of it with a will, so with much shuffling of feet, we began to address the passers-by. My congregation, after five minutes of valiant effort, consisted of two pigeons and a lamp-post! And the only reason they hung around was because the pigeons couldn't understand and the lamp-post couldn't move. I stopped in no little confusion. Where was the glory? Where was God's promised help?

But God would not let me go. So a few days later I decided to try one more time, saying to God, 'I am not doing this for my health, but to reach people. If it's not going to reach people I'm not interested and I'm sure you're not interested either. So if you really want me to continue this then please have somebody stop today and show a real interest.' John and I gave it one more go and this time people stopped and talked.

Over the course of that summer people were saved who are still going on with Christ today. I was launched into a ministry of open-air preaching which was to continue for the next nine years. John Goodfellow went on to Holland and introduced this style of evangelism there, a style which soon became a major feature in YWAM's summer of service programmes and led to hundreds coming into the kingdom. The ripples went on; all because God had pressurised us, as only he can do, into boldness in evangelism.

'I'm a fool for Jesus; whose fool are you?' is a well-known little evangelical phrase that has much to recommend it. If our first concern is to protect our reputation, we will never take those risky steps of faith. Why, we might be embarrassed by our failure! But unrisky Christianity is boring Christianity and, worse, ineffective Christianity.

Catherine Booth, co-founder with her husband of the Salvation Army, was so timid in her early years that she considered it a triumph worthy of a special mention in a letter that she, at the age of twenty-five, had actually prayed out loud at a prayer meeting. (Perhaps some of you can relate to this!) Six years later, shy Mrs Booth was listening to her husband preach to his packed Methodist Church when the Lord urged her to stand up before the whole congregation and share some of what God had been doing in her life recently. She knew this would be a blessing to people, but she was afraid. She relates her inner turmoil:

And the Devil said, "Besides, you are not prepared to speak. You will look like a fool and have nothing to say." He made a mistake! He (the devil) overdid himself for once! It was that word that settled it. I said, "Ah! This is just the point. I have never yet been willing to be a fool for Christ, now I will be one."

With that she went up to the front to tell her husband

she wanted to say something for Jesus. William, flab-bergasted but delighted, promptly seized the initiative and announced that his wife would be preaching at the evening service! So started a preaching career that brought thousands into the kingdom, a preaching career so dynamic that some of her gentlemen admirers offered to build a church just for her which would be larger than the 5,000-seater Tabernacle of the celebrated Baptist preacher, Charles Spurgeon.[5] All because she stepped past her fear and did not care whether she would be thought a fool. 'I'm a fool for Jesus; whose fool are you?'

Be willing to make mistakes

'The man who never made a mistake never made anything.'

If we are not evangelising because we are waiting to get to a place where we won't make mistakes, then rest assured—we will never evangelise. Mistakes are part of life. We learn by making mistakes. Training can minimise mistakes, but can never guarantee us against mistakes. We learn by doing and, of necessity, our first attempts are going to be inexpert and clumsy. But it is only by pressing on through this first stage that we can improve. When you were first learning to ride a bicycle you wobbled and wavered, but you persevered and eventually got it. You did not learn by studying thick tomes from the library on *The Theory of Bicycling* or *All You Ever Wanted to Know About Two-Wheeled Vehicles But Were Afraid to Ask*. No, you just went out and did it and you learned.

Some people are hyper-critical of the ways others do evangelism. They know exactly where others are doing it wrong. They remind me of the story about D L Moody who once talked to a critic of his mass evangelism crusade techniques. Moody asked the critic how he did evangelism and the man said he didn't, to which Moody's response was, 'Well, I like the way I do evangelism better than the way you don't do it.'

Don't wait for the perfect method of evangelism to come along. There will always be something to criticise in any approach. C T Studd, nineteenth-century missionary to three different continents, encouraged his wife not to wilt under people's criticism by remembering the tale of the miller's donkey. A miller, son and donkey went to the market. The miller rode the donkey all the way and people exclaimed, 'Cruel man, riding himself and making his son walk.' So he got down and his son rode. Then people slanged, 'What a lazy son for riding while his poor old father walks.' Then both father and son rode, and people then said, 'Cruelty to animals, poor donkey.' So they got down and carried the donkey on a pole, but folks said, 'Here are two asses carrying another ass.' Then all three walked and people said, 'What fools to have a donkey and not to ride it.'

Fear of criticism and fear of making mistakes will freeze us up. *God's Frozen People* is a book title that aptly tags the church of Jesus Christ. But Jesus was no sedate dreamer who said, 'Come to me and I will make you comfortable.' He challenged his disciples down to their socks (adapted for sandals on special offer at Marcus and Spencerium's). They did things they had never done before and, quite naturally, on the way they made mistakes and encountered failure. 'Why couldn't we drive it out?' they asked (Mt 17:19). They tried; they failed; they learned.

I can well recall going in 1973 to one of the hotels used by the young, Western travellers in Kabul, Afghanistan, with the firm intention to evangelise. I had just been greatly enthused by one of Arthur Blessitt's books in which he told of his going into a prison visiting room and, not knowing what else to do, had simply stood up and began preaching. As a consequence, one young man had given his life to Christ. Convinced that this approach held much promise, I hit the hippy hotels. I finally found some likely victims in a small, two-bed room wherein lay two hapless hippies. I boldly strode to the centre of the room, cleared my throat and announced to those gathered on this most holy occasion, 'I am a Christian and have come to talk about Christ.' At that, one devotee rolled over, faced the wall and groaned loudly. Pain and disgust were what I heard and I think more of the latter. I soundly concluded that the other man was the one for me. Great was my disappointment upon going over and speaking to him, for it turned out that his agreeableness was founded on the fact that he didn't understand a single word of English. After a few moments of mutual beaming and nodding, I beat a hasty retreat.

You win some, you lose some. But if you are not willing to lose any, you won't win any either. 'Nothing ventured, nothing gained,' is a saying which through repetition has gained much in triteness and lost nothing in truthfulness.

Don't worry if you feel inadequate...you are!

Most of us feel terribly inadequate when it comes to the subject of evangelism. We feel we'll probably embarrass God horribly and embarrass ourselves, and we are not sure which is worse.

Surely the early apostles had to struggle with exactly the same sense of inadequacy? They were expert, experienced fishermen, not expert apostles. But they were supported and enabled to go on because their trust was not in their own skills but in Jesus' promise, 'I will make you fishers of men' (Mt 4:19).

Hear that promise loud and clear, and claim it for yourself. Don't muddle it like my daughter who, upon coming home from pre-school one day, said, 'Daddy, Jesus gave us a great promise. He said, "Come follow me and I will make you...fish and chips." ' Fishers of men is the promise. Jesus said he would take us on and begin this moulding process. The responsibility lies with him. And what God promises he fulfils.

God uses all sorts in evangelism. I shall never forget one unlikely candidate for 'Mr Evangelism'. I met Geoff in 1972 at the teahouse ministry in Kabul, Afghanistan, which a team of us ran under the leadership of Floyd McClung. Geoff came through to watch a film, but was so wide open to God that by the end of the evening he had given his heart to Jesus. This gentle little Geordie won all our hearts with his quiet and self-effacing character, but he never betrayed a hint of dynamic ministry gifts that would lead us to pick him out saying, 'Now there goes the next Billy Graham in miniature.' He never displayed any of the signs associated with the evangelistic superstar, ie loudness, pushiness, gregarious and boisterous personality, spookily quavering prayer voice and, last but not least, he was definitely too skinny ever to be able to thump anyone properly with his Bible.

Is this really evangelist raw material, you ask yourself? Exactly my question two years later when reports of his goings-on in India and Nepal started to filter back to me. First it was letters about going off to the hill tribes of Nepal by jeep to preach the gospel; then it was reports of meetings in huts where 'the presence of God so filled the place that three Sherpa [Buddhist] guides fell on their faces in awe'; then it was a 'stadium in Patna, India, with thousands coming every night to receive healing and

44

salvation'. 'This was Geoff? Shy and reticent Geoff?' would be my incredulous response. Yes, God can use any of us.

Our sense of inadequacy is heightened by three 'worry feeders': our fear of rejection, a sense of inferiority, an attitude of defeatism. If we let these three attitudes run rampant in our lives we will be paralysed in our desire to be a witness for Christ.

Worry magnifies the problems and, unsatisfied with this, invents them when they are not there. You may have heard Mark Twain's quip: 'I've had many troubles in my life but most of them have never happened to me.' Too true. Let's be on our guard against the following:

Fear of rejection

A fear of rejection is, to a certain extent, a totally natural reaction. God made us for love; not only to give love but to want love and to need love. When we enter a situation where love is withheld from us we recoil from the situation. Completely understandable. We are not meant to like the situation. God doesn't like it.

Applying this to evangelism, we know that either due to misunderstanding or wilful rebellion many people will not receive the gospel with welcoming arms. We know that many will not receive us, the gospel messengers, with open arms. We don't like this prospect. Nobody likes rejection.

In my memory, my first ever evangelistic foray is not distinguished by glowing joy but by abject terror. I had only been a Christian a short while when it was decided that I was now ready to share my faith. So, with a small group of other Christians on a similar mission, we headed into downtown Kabul—straight for the dreaded 'Sigis', one of the main 'freak'[6] hangouts, a real mecca for the drug traffic. We trudged up the dingy staircase and entered a room which was bare except for six rope beds where our current targets lay. My eyes rolled as I viewed the five-foot-high drawing on the far wall. It depicted an oversized skull on top of an emaciated body with one long arm wielding an oversized syringe plunged into a bulging vein popping out of the bone-thin arm. The memory ever lives with me. Under the watchful, baleful eyes of this, the room's guardian, I went up to one of the reclining German freaks and made my first attempts at sharing my faith. Nothing much happened and I am sure I muttered complete inanities, but the point is that I had begun to break the fear barrier. 'The journey of a thousand miles starts with a single step.' My journey had begun.

Fear of rejection is natural. It is only when we allow this to dominate our lives that it becomes sinful. Courage is not the absence of the emotion of fear. Courage is, despite the presence of fear, proceeding with our duty.

We can have the courage we need by feeding on God's word. If you want to have a courageous attitude dwell on en-courage-ing thoughts. Specifically, dwell on God's promise of total acceptance; he never rejects us. And if the most important being in the universe accepts us, why should we be bothered over much by what others think of us? 'If God is for us, who can be against us?' (Rom 8:31). Secondly, dwell on the glory of the gospel; how it is such a total provision for people's very real eternal needs. A fresh realisation of this will do more for our courage than a battery of cannons behind us because 'perfect love drives out fear' (1 Jn 4:18). The more I am looking to be a blessing to you, the less I am concerned that your reaction be a blessing to me. Your rejection or acceptance of me becomes secondary to your rejection or acceptance of the living God.

Sense of inferiority

I mentioned that another worry feeder was a sense of inferiority, a proneness to feeling intimidated by the surface sophistication of the world around us. Can the old-fashioned gospel with its simple message of the rugged cross really stand tall before a glittering, fast-paced world geared to state-of-the-art truth? During a series of open-air, evangelistic meetings I had organised in central London's Covent Garden, I was battling with feeling intimidated. Here we were with our simple message, simple testimonies and slapped-together dramas in the midst of this temple of trendiness through which the fashionable young, draped in a painful air of contrived casualness, trooped in all their splendour.

We had very consciously to reject this lie of inferiority before we could go on with a free spirit. God, the Maker of the heavens and earth, inferior? The gospel message, which revolutionises individuals for eternity, inferior to Madison Avenue glitz? Ridiculous! We had to meditate and pray and worship in this vein and only then were we fit to go out and share the good news.

If we had succumbed to this sense of inferiority I never would have met Ruth and James. They were strolling through Covent Garden and came across our open air. I engaged them in conversation and soon we were talking about Jesus. Going through marriage strains as they were, they were completely open to hear about what Jesus had done and could do for them. It was my joy to lead them through the sinner's prayer right there on Covent Garden's plazza. A few days later we contacted them by phone and they excitedly related how God was healing their marriage and how they had met Christians at work. They had gone along with their new-found Christian friends to their local church and were happily beginning to fit in there. All this because we had refused to succumb to the lie of inferiority. Don't be frozen, act like God's chosen!

Sophisticated defeatism

The last worry feeder is an outlook on life that always sees why an action will fail, but never why it will succeed. It's a defeatism that is expert in the problems, but a novice in solutions. If we do not have faith for the success of a venture we will never get started in it. Indeed, it would be foolish to start something we know is going to fail. We do not evangelise for the exercise. We do it to see people won to Jesus.

In 1984 I led a team from Britain to the Los Angeles Olympic games—not the official sports team, you understand, but an evangelism team. Our team took on a wide variety of evangelistic locations. One Tuesday we decided to head for an out-of-town reservoir which, reportedly, was popular with the locals mid-week. Upon arriving we discovered a paltry scattering of people spread far and wide up and down the beach.

I was the leader so everybody looked to me with the obvious question, 'What do we do now?' Maintaining an outer appearance of calm assurance while groaning inwardly, I weakly suggested we should pray. Good start! In prayer we thought we should go around to each little group of bathers with our thirty-strong team and offer to do a song and a drama. They could hardly refuse seeing as there were thirty of us and two of them. Friendship evangelism!

We made quite a sight. Totally unprepared for the beach in our dresses and rolled up long trousers, white skin untouched by the sun, four-cornered handkerchiefs proudly perched on our heads (clearly we had to represent Great Britain properly) we paraded among the bronzed Californians coolly lazing in the sun beneath oil and Ray-Bans.

I am afraid we rather startled the pair of lounging lifeguards who were never trained in crowd control. Their eyes widened as they beheld this outlandishly attired thirty-strong crew trudging towards them with such determination. When asked if they would like a song imported from Britain they concluded they had better humour us and agreed to listen. We went through our mini-performance of one song and one drama, dropped off two of our team and moved on to the next batch of unsuspecting victims. This we did until our entire group of thirty had been split up. Conversations were going on up and down the beach. I must admit that I wasn't full of faith about this approach, but doing something imperfectly was better than doing nothing perfectly.

Two hours later, when we got everybody back together again for a report, we found that during the course of the afternoon six people had committed their lives to Christ! It had turned out to be the best day of our whole two-week outreach.

One of our girls had grown so hot in the blazing sun that she ignored her lack of a bathing costume and simply waded into the lake up past her knees. Sighing contentedly, she found herself standing next to a Mexican woman holding a two-year-old child. They were soon in earnest conversation and in no time were praying for the woman to receive Christ. Our eager evangelist was by this time holding the infant who, at this delicate moment, was raising the water level of the lake in the supremely unselfconscious style common to children the world over.

We had gone out like lambs and came back like lions.

A magnificent afternoon. But it never would have happened if we had let defeatism grip our souls. Let God be God in our lives and let him turn all sorts of situations around for good. Enter into the rest of faith.

Here's a little prayer I was once taught, and which I often use when going into evangelistic situations which do not initially look promising:

> I can't.
> You can.
> Thank you that you will.

Battle of faiths

In all of this we need to realise that there is a battle of faiths going on around us. The battle is over whether the unbeliever believes what he believes more than I believe what I believe. Whose faith is stronger—the Christian's faith in the gospel or the sceptic's faith in his scepticism?

The realisation of this battle came forcefully to me over the course of two weekend open airs. I was down in London's Portobello Market and every time I stood up to proclaim the gospel I cringed inside, belying my outward bravado. Later on, as people prayed for me, I became aware that I was struggling with feeling ashamed of the gospel. I also became aware that this shame came from the fact that, very subtly, I was allowing what I knew to be going through people's minds to infiltrate my mind; not so much thoughts like, 'What rubbish,' but thoughts like, 'Why can't you just keep your beliefs to yourself? Why shout? Why get so excited? Calm down, me old son.'

It was an attack on my faith; not on the truthfulness of the gospel (that would be too obvious and immediately rejected), but on the importance of the gospel. They felt

Christianity was nice but irrelevant. I knew they felt this way and was allowing it to dampen my zeal. In practice, they were believing what they believed more than I believed what I believed. The battle of faiths was on and they were winning... for the moment. As it became clear to me what was going on I was able to knock this particular device on the head by asking for prayer and by affirming in the face of this lie that the gospel was both true and important. The next time I stood up in the open air I no longer cringed.

Our mind is the Devil's battleground. Jesus said the Enemy exercises a ministry. His ministry is in complete contrast to the ministry of the Holy Spirit who has a ministry of truth. The Devil has a lying ministry—'When he lies, he speaks his native language, for he is a liar and the father of lies' (Jn 8:44). In this passage in John, Jesus focuses on two of the Enemy's activities—lying and murdering—and his main emphasis, his greater concern, is on the lying rather than the murdering. Surprising perhaps, but not when we realise that the only way the Enemy can introduce death into our lives is through lying. Death is the outcome, but lying is the main tool. It was so in the Garden of Eden and it is so today.

We will never enter into boldness and overcome feelings of inadequacy, rejection and inferiority if we are unaware of how to foil the Devil in his lying ministry. God's three simple steps to defeat these lies are prayer, belief and action.

We need to be fellowshipping with the Lord in prayer. Then we will be close to his heart and we will not be easily duped by the Enemy.

We need to believe God's word. We combat lies with truth and God's word is truth. To the Enemy's, 'Did God say?' we reply, 'Yes, he did say.'

But we also need to act. Once, in my daily quiet time,

I had been meditating on the story of David leaping and dancing unashamedly before the ark of God. His wife despised his behaviour and had rebuked him sarcastically saying, 'How the king of Israel has distinguished himself today, disrobing in the sight of the slave girls of his servants as any vulgar fellow would!' I was so impressed with David's abandonment to God, his consequent refusal to stand on ceremony, the steely determination with which he responded saying, 'I will celebrate before the Lord. I will become even more undignified than this, and I will be humiliated in my own eyes' (2 Sam 6:16–22). I prayed then and there that God would make me more like David, determined to glorify God no matter what the cost in terms of personal reputation. That was the prayer and believing part. God then provided the opportunity for action.

That afternoon I went into a builders' merchants' yard for some house supplies. Now, builders' merchants are very macho places. They are places for men, not soft-handed, lily-white clerks blinking behind thick bifocals, but men toughened through hours spent outdoors in hard labour. Football, booze and girls are all acceptable subjects for conversation; perfume, ballet and God are not. The proprietor of this particular shop was new and, as was obvious from the way he was swearing, was trying hard to be accepted by the lads. Into this atmosphere enters your innocent YWAM missionary, having just prayed for the boldness of David. The trouble with praying is that God answers!

The proprietor wheeled around at my entrance and boomed out, 'Hello, Mr American [he knew me from before]! What can I get you? What are you doing over here in England anyway?' Here was my opportunity for boldness. What did your hero do? Why, he stalled, of course. These are the moments of truth. God has set up the situation and now it's up to you. You feel much like a swimmer contemplating a cold pool, shivering from the side. The hard part is diving in. Once you are in you are too numb to feel uncomfortable.

I asked for a quarter pound of nails to give me time to think. I thought, 'If I say I am a missionary that will sound too tame. I need something with a bit more teeth.' So I said, 'God sent me over...to do Christian work.' Once said, it was easy. After all, I was too numb to feel it! Once in the pool we find it isn't so bad after all and are a little ashamed of all the fuss we made up on the poolside. In fact, it is exhilarating sharing about Jesus. This is part of what we were made for—'You shall be my witnesses.'

'God sent me over....' That set them back a little bit, but as I shared it rather casually and didn't whip out my ten-pound Bible while glaring the John-the-Baptist-Franco-Zeffirelli-prophetic glare, they took it much as if I had said, 'My boss sent me over' (completely true!).

People will take their cue from us. If we share our faith in such a way that presumes it is the most natural and intelligent thing in the world then people will feel this and are more likely to accept it as such. If we are relaxed, they will be relaxed. As it is so important, we shall devote the whole of the next chapter looking at this area of 'naturalness' in evangelism.

4

Hang Loose, Baby

'Try to be natural.' That's like saying, 'Don't worry,' to a neurotic. Nevertheless, being natural and being ourselves is important in evangelism. This is not meant as an excuse for laziness nor as an excuse for just doing what we feel like doing. Someone once said, 'Be yourself but be the best self you can be.' That puts it about right.

Jesus was totally natural. He did not speak to individuals with a put-on, quavery voice, nor did he wear a mystically vacant stare as he looked out over the multitudes, nor did he walk Palestine's dusty roads with sanctimonious, delicate steps whining, 'Oh these roads are so filthy! Tut, tut! Up in heaven we use shiny gold. Such a better class of person there.' Jesus was down to earth; nothing put-on about him. He talked, walked and looked like an ordinary man. That's why ordinary people were comfortable with him. That's why irreligious sinners—prostitutes, swindling taxmen, rough-and-ready thieves—could sit at his feet and listen to him, invite him for dinner, ask him for help. This they would never have done with the laboriously religious Pharisees, too busy straining out gnats and swallowing camels (silly pastime!) to relax and be human.

Here are three bits of advice which will enable us to be more natural in our evangelism: just be who you are, let God convert people and don't expect to take everybody from A to Z.

Just be who you are

Do not think that evangelism has to do with being a certain type of personality to which you must conform. There is no such thing as an 'evangelistic personality'. If you are a quiet type, just share in your quiet way. If you are loud and boisterous, just share in your loud and boisterous way. God comes best through you when you are who he had made you to be. Just be who you are. It's hard to be anybody else.

Granted, Billy Graham effectively preaches to the crowds by impressively thumping his big leather-bound Bible as, with set jaw and glittering eye, he sonorously declares that 'the Bible says...'. Fine, but don't you go and painstakingly rehearse these same anointed gestures and voice inflections in front of your mirror. You might wear out too many Bibles in the process.

I shall always remember Ken Korol as an example of a man who was content to let the love of God to come through his God-given personality. Ken was a complete 'straight' among all us 'freaks' there in Afghanistan. He was from a slightly older generation, had never been part of the drugs and counter-culture set and did everything wrong in terms of surface appearance and dress—short hair, perma-press trousers and tidy white shirts. Did that mean he could not identify or communicate? Not on

your nelly. Ken Korol loved people and love communi-
cates.

Once I went with Ken on one of his witnessing rounds
through several of Kabul's freak hotels. We came upon
six young people sitting in a circle. We joined them and
Ken began sharing. In the midst of Ken's talking a
glassy-eyed German took out his hash pipe, lit up and
passed it around to eagerly grasping hands. It made its
way around the circle to Ken who, without batting an
eyelash, quietly declined and continued talking.

Even though he had never been a part of it, dope
smoking never threw Ken off his stride. He saw people's
eternity more than their temporal actions. Whether they
were businessmen or hippies was of no concern to him;
they all needed Jesus. Ken was not put off by people's
differences and so people were not put off by his differences.

One young German called Dieter came to our ministry centre to try to kick his morphine addiction. As he
went 'cold turkey' Ken would be there for hours, kneel-
ing at the end of his bed and praying that Dieter would
make it. Ken prayed that man right through so that he
hardly had any withdrawal pains. Not only that, he
prayed him right through to the kingdom. Today, that
German, who had left home with a failed, incompleted
secondary education, is serving God in Germany with a
master's degree in theology.

Ken Korol did not try to be someone he was not. He
was sure God could use him just as he was. So it should
be for us. We do not have to try to be more this, less that
or better anything when we go into 'witnessing mode'.
God uses us as we are.

Let God convert people

Let God convert people; he's better at it than we are. Converting people is not our job but the job of the Holy Spirit. As soon as we take on the ultimate responsibility and feel that we have to see this person through, we become tense, strident and pushy.

Arie, converted from being a gang-leader in the Dutch town of Apeldoorn, was very enthusiastic to see people saved. He went out on the streets with his zealous band of Christians to collar people for Jesus. He would not let his contacts go until they had kneeled with him on the streets and recited a prayer. Knowing his background, most decided discretion was the better part of valour and became suddenly religious. But Arie would be sorely disappointed the next day to find his 'converts' still frequenting their old haunts and still pursuing their sinful lifestyles. 'Conversions' that originate with us end with us. As soon as we leave the scene, the conversion evaporates. They are not real conversions, but are like the elderly lady who once said to a friend of mine, 'Oh, don't worry about me, sonny. I gave my life to Billy Graham years ago.'

Relax when you are sharing your faith with people. Just give people what God gives you to give them. Trust the Holy Spirit in you to guide you. Don't force issues beyond which the Holy Spirit is forcing them. Find out what the Holy Spirit is pressing and press that. The witness is just a midwife assisting in a birth. We assist, we don't make it all happen.

There is no need to talk endlessly when sharing your faith with someone. Some think that effective witnessing is like a private preaching session, with your contact as the congregation. No, you are having a conversation. Conversations are two way. You need to listen as well as speak. Then you can tailor your talk according to what the person is telling you and to what the Holy Spirit is telling you.

Relax and let the Holy Spirit guide you as to what aspect of God you should be sharing. You have not necessarily failed in your communication just because you never mentioned the cross or talked about the blood. Sometimes people need to hear about another aspect of the character of God. See how Jesus approached the invalid by the pool in John 5. He healed him and, without preaching even a hint of a sermon, departed. Not only did Jesus neglect to tell him the way of salvation, he did not even tell him who he was (see verse 13). You won't find this witnessing technique in any book on witnessing!

Can you imagine Jesus panicking because he had missed his opportunity to share the good news? Hardly. He was content to follow the lead of the Spirit. Afterwards, Jesus sought out the man and explained things to him. Even here Jesus broke our contemporary rules of witnessing in that what he said was real 'turn or burn' stuff: 'Stop sinning or something worse may happen to you' (v 14). Didn't he know you can't say things like that to people?

Jesus' witnessing had a wondrous blend of grace and truth; not altogether surprising in someone who was described as 'full of grace and truth' (Jn 1:14). Witnessing like Jesus means witnessing with both grace and truth. Truth without grace can be hard and harmful. Grace without truth can be spineless and crowd-pleasing.

Love and truth have been likened to sodium and chlorine.

Sodium is an extremely active element found naturally in combined form; it always links itself to another element. Chlorine is the poisonous gas that gives bleach its offensive odour. When sodium and chlorine are combined the result is sodium chloride—common table salt—the substance we use to preserve meat and bring out flavour....

Grace without truth is flighty, sometimes blind, willing to combine with various doctrines. On the other hand, truth by itself can be offensive, sometimes even poisonous. Spoken without love, it can turn people away from the gospel. When grace and truth are combined...we have what Jesus called 'the salt of the earth'.[7]

It is not only the truth we tell, but the graciousness we exhibit which is a witness to the King. But there is no way we can be gracious if we shoulder God's responsibility for seeing people converted. We can't afford to be gracious! If we let up for a moment there won't be anyone around to bring conviction down on their heads. We have to push, push, push. And now here is some rigorous logic: if we push, people feel pushed. People do not like to be pushed. Push trolleys, push buttons, but don't push people.

I recall one incensed lady I met outside the Santa Anita racetrack during the LA Olympics. As I was trying to witness to her, she bitterly related an encounter with a Jehovah's Witness on her doorstep who, when she wanted to finish the discussion and go inside, grabbed her arm and would not let her go. She ended up yelling at him, 'Let me go or I'll sue you.' That is not the kind of impression we want to leave people with. People appreciate graciousness.

One Saturday evening at an open air in London's Leicester Square I met a young couple on their way to the theatre. The young man had only recently had his interest in the New Testament rekindled and, consequently, we had a most animated and productive discussion. After forty-five minutes it became obvious to me that we had finished what the Holy Spirit wanted doing for that time. At the same time another Christian joined

our little group and started up a new discussion. I could
see that this young couple now wanted to get off to their
theatre, but were too polite to say so. No problem. I butt
in on my Christian colleague, who was only just warming
to his theme, and said, 'Listen, I'm sure you need to get
off now to your show. You can leave if you want to. Why
don't we exchange addresses so we can get in touch
later.' With visible relief they agreed and amicably we
parted company. That couple will have left with an
impression that not only are Christian people with firm
convictions but people with gracious sensitivities, and
that can only glorify our Lord who was 'full of grace and
truth'.

Don't expect to take everybody from A to Z

How many of us were converted the first time we heard
the gospel? When I ask that in a public meeting it is
usually about 5% of those present. Conversion is a process that happens over time. Jesus told one young man
that he was 'not far from the kingdom' (Mk 12:34), the
implication being that some who are unconverted are
further and some are closer. People go through a process, moving from far from the kingdom to close to the
kingdom, when they undergo conversion. Of course, this
process can take place quickly within the course of one
meeting or it can occur slowly over the course of years.
One communications and marketing expert, Dr J Engel,
has even broken down this 'spiritual decision process'
into eight identifiable steps beginning with 'some aware-
ness of the Supreme Being', through 'a grasp of the
personal implications of the gospel', and ending with
'repentance and faith'.[8]

One day Jesus was walking through Samaria, commenting to his disciples on the harvest of souls that was

all around them. He added: 'Thus the saying "One sows and another reaps" is true. I sent you to reap what you have not worked for. Others have done the hard work, and you have reaped the benefits of their labour' (Jn 4:37–38). In other words, Jesus was saying that others had taken the people from A to T, but the disciples would take them from T to Z. That's the fun part, seeing people come right through to a relationship with the living God. The 'hard work' is seeing people move from being far to God to closer to God without actual conversion. It is hard because it is less satisfying. We all want to be there when the seed brings forth fruit. Sitting around and watching the leaves grow inch by inch, day by day, is a whole lot less enthralling.

However, no plant gets to the fruit-bearing stage without first going through the initial, mundane growing stages. Jesus was saying just this when he likened the kingdom of God to a seed that 'sprouts and grows, though he does not know how. All by itself the soil produces corn—first the stalk, then the ear, then the full kernel in the ear. As soon as the grain is ripe, he puts the sickle to it, because the harvest has come' (Mk 4:27–29).

Danny Lehman, YWAM evangelist in Hawaii, talks about the 'gospel belt' all witnesses carry with them. This belt has a pouch for gospel seeds, a fork for clearing weeds, pruning shears for nipping off unnecessary growth, a sickle for harvesting. Some people we meet simply need the gospel seed planted, some need pruning, some are ready for harvesting. The trick is to discern where the person is in their spiritual odyssey and then to use the appropriate tool. It is a waste of time to be planting seeds in people's hearts when they are like overripe grain begging to be picked. Get out the sickle. But to be wildly running around with our sickle swinging eagerly at everything in sight is equally bad gardening technique. The zealous evangelist bearing down on some spindly, half-developed plant with his gleaming sickle does not end up with ripe grain to the glory of God, he simply ends up with a dead plant.

Successful evangelism is not only getting 'decisions' for the Lord, it is moving people along a little closer to God. We may feel disappointed because we only had a good talk with someone without actually seeing them come through to faith in Christ. We mustn't despair. It is through such steps that each of us came to know Christ for ourselves.

Back in 1971 when I was the 'happy hippy from Hillsborough'[9] I came across some dreaded 'Jesus freaks'.[10] I had always regarded Jesus freaks as very narrow-minded people who could not appreciate others' viewpoints and who never left other people alone (in fact, like me now!)—definitely to be avoided at all costs. But on this day I was left manning a booth advertising yoga and meditation on a university campus when two of them came up to me. Cornered! Within two minutes they could see that I was not in the least open to hearing the gospel so, instead of arguing ('scriptures at ten paces'), they suggested, 'Can we say a quick prayer together?'

'Sure,' I said. 'It's the same God we worship anyway.'

Biting their lips they simply bowed their heads, prayed, and left with a good-natured wave. I recorded the event in my diary and promptly forgot about it.

Nine months later I was half-way around the world in India. Hiram Hyratt, the elderly Indian who had first stopped me on the streets of Mussoorie, had introduced me to Geoff Williams, an English missionary involved in the charismatic renewal. It was through Geoff that I really took my Christian search further. One afternoon I went over to his house for a chat. I entered his living room and plonked myself on the settee waiting for him to appear. As it happened, I was carrying my diary with me. In throwing myself down on the settee the diary had fallen open. I looked down and my eye immediately caught the little PS penned at the bottom of the page. With a jolt I read, 'Today did a few moments of prayer with some Christians. What will this come to?' It was my note on meeting the two Jesus freaks.

What would come of it indeed! The answer is that it had come to this: I was reading the Scriptures for the first time in my life, going to prayer meetings, reading Christian books (I had bought my first Christian book, one I deemed 'safe' and unfanatical: *Mere Christianity* by CS Lewis) and had met Christians who could really challenge me with Christ. In short, I was considering Christ. After a week of pursuing this new-found Christian interest I, still hanging on to my Eastern mysticism and not yet a believer in Christ, decided I must go back to my ashram (a sort of yogic monastery). Disappointed, some of the Christians saw me off from the depot.

But God was not finished with me. Responsibility for conversion rests with him. Crammed into the little taxi making its way to the train station I chocked my past week down as an 'interesting experience' to be filed, and then let my thoughts drift on to the details of my upcoming travel. Where should I change trains? And what should I order for dinner tonight? Suddenly, like a bolt, the thought flashed through my mind, shaking me to my roots, '*Wow*, it's *true*. It's really true.' Numbed and overwhelmed with my discovery, I could only idiotically repeat this over and over to myself. I knew instinctively that 'it' referred to Christianity. Bouncing along in an ancient, battered taxicab filled with buzzing flies and turbaned Sikhs, I was being born again by the Spirit of God! So began my Christian life.

The point that needs making here is that to this day

those two Californian Jesus freaks don't know any of this. To them, that yoga devotee was hard and stubborn. Quite possibly they returned home with a feeling of failure, a feeling they had not accomplished anything for God. They could not even console themselves with having had a good talk with me. All they did was pray. But their prayer was part of the chain God used to bring me to himself. God answered that prayer. They were successful in that they had played their God-given part in my spiritual journey.

Be content to be part of God's plan and leave the overall picture to him. Let God convert people. Let God be God and then you can be free just to be yourself.

5

Friendship Evangelism

'People don't care how much we know until they know how much we care,' says Floyd McClung. Floyd calls this approach 'friendship evangelism'. Friendship evangelism means that we move beyond a formal, professional relationship of evangeliser and evangelised to a warm, human relationship where we really care for those we share with. They are not targets but human beings.

The apostle Paul puts it in a nutshell when he writes, 'We loved you so much that we were delighted to share with you not only the gospel of God but our lives as well' (1 Thess 2:8). This kind of evangelism has credibility and authority because it has reality. But reality is not only rewarding, it is costly.

Geoff and Pauline Williams were a couple who learned this in a very personal way. Geoff and Pauline had been called by God to serve in India with Christian Literature Crusade (CLC). They left England at the end of the 1960s and went up to the hills of north India where, in Mussoorie, they took over the CLC bookshop.

One day God spoke strongly to them out of Romans 5:5 which reads, 'God has poured out his love into our hearts by the Holy Spirit, whom he has given us.' God would not let them get away from this verse. They began to make it their constant prayer.

A few weeks after all this had begun Geoff was wandering through the Mussoorie bazaar, head bowed, earnestly praying this scripture into his life, when he espied a dirty pair of feet in leather sandals directly in front of him. His eyes travelled up past the thin, cotton trousers, past the beaded vest to the granny glasses and long, scraggly hair of a Western hippy. Geoff was just about to rush past when the Lord prompted him, 'I thought you wanted to learn to love.'

'Yes, Lord, but I'm here to reach the Indians, not Westerners. Besides, I'm as square as a cube. What could I say to help these hippies?'

'Can you love them?'

'Uh, well, Lord....' And so the argument went until, finally, God won. Geoff sidled up alongside the stranger saying, 'Hello, my name is Geoff.'

'Ach, I am Olaf from Denmark. You want to smoke some ganja with me? Come on in to my room.'

'Well, I'll come in but no ganja for me, thanks.'

Discarded cauliflower heads and beadie butts (Indian cigarettes made from raw tobacco) were strewn about the floor amidst copies of *The Tibetan Book of the Dead* and *Steppenwolf*. As great blue waves of choking smoke rolled over him, Geoff shared his testimony. Olaf listened disinterestedly, eyes roving round the room, muttering, 'Sure, sure.'

Groaning inwardly, Geoff protested, 'Lord, I've done everything I can and nothing seems to be getting through.'

'You haven't loved him yet.'

'I can't, Lord. I can't get involved and bring someone like this home. I've got a wife and three little children. What will they say if I turn up with him on my doorstep? You don't seem to realise the problems this could cause.'

'Conversation finished, Geoff.'

With that, Geoff resigned himself to his fate and asked Olaf if he would like to come home with him. Well, Geoff had never raised the dead before, but that was the closest he ever came. Olaf, previously listless and apathetic, sprang to his feet saying, 'Do you really mean that?' and within minutes he was standing at attention near the door with his few belongings bundled up and ready to go.

Geoff, meanwhile, was earnestly praying for grace to come down upon his wife for this little surprise he was going to bring home. On their arrival, Pauline, in her usual gracious way, welcomed them warmly, though she did rather firmly suggest that perhaps Olaf would like a bath before sitting down to dinner with the family.

They put him to bed in the room next to theirs, a room only partitioned off from theirs by a head high wall. Through this gap between the wall and the ceiling poured Olaf's cigarette smoke—and Olaf smoked like a fiend through much of the night. Spluttering and coughing, Geoff and Pauline lulled themselves to sleep by quietly but firmly repeating, 'The love of God is shed abroad in our hearts. The love of God is shed abroad in our hearts,' and so on. The next morning Olaf packed up and left without making a commitment to the Lord. This did not mean that nothing positive happened. As Geoff says, 'He didn't come to Christ; Christ had come to us.' God had started a fresh work in their hearts and was teaching them to love as he loved.

Geoff prayed to God, 'Lord, if you really want us to reach these people, then you are going to have to bring

them to us. I am not going to go out and look for them.'
And God did just that. Over the course of the next three
years God brought over one hundred Western travellers
from twenty-two different nations through Geoff and
Pauline's home. Many of these made deep commitments
to the Lord and have gone on to serve him around the
world.

One Daniel Ruland, met begging for food in rags
before a Hindu temple, went on to travel around the
world on Operation Mobilisation's ship 'The Logos'
using his ventriloquist skills to preach the gospel to thousands of children.

Another went on to become a leader in an international missionary organisation, Youth With A Mission, and is in fact the writer of this book.

Geoff and Pauline themselves were greatly changed
through contact with hippies from so many nations. Not
only did God deepen their love, but he broadened their
vision—the whole world became their parish. In time,
God launched them into a ministry of encouraging and
equipping Christian ministries throughout the Far East.

God used Geoff and Pauline because they were willing to give not only the gospel but their very lives. Giving
is costly. They lived on a faith budget where they did not
know where that week's grocery money was coming
from. It was with a gulp and a prayer that they often sat
down with a famished long-haired guest who, on spotting
Marmite, jam and meat, would yelp with delight saying,
'I haven't seen Western food for months!' and then
proceed to shovel down half of that week's carefully
preserved shopping. On top of that, not all of the missionary force was convinced they were acting with the
wisdom and circumspection called for in a foreign missionary.

Some asked them incredulously, 'You don't use the

same loo, do you? You might catch VD! You're crazy.'
But God didn't think they were crazy, nor did the many
young Westerners who found new life through their
lives. Evangelism is more than giving God's words, it is
giving our lives.

Friendship key

Here are some statistics for you to consider. See if you
draw the same conclusions I do.

1. Lyle Schaller, a much respected parish consultant
and church planner in the United States, did some research
into why church members joined one particular congregation over another. He came up with these figures:

5–10%: 'We just walked in on our own.'

15–20%: referred to the pastor as the primary
reason.

70–80%: referred to friendship and kinship ties as
being the primary reason. (In rapidly growing congregations friendship ties were more
frequently cited than kinship ties.)[11]

2. The Institute of American Church Growth in Pasadena, California, asked 14,000 lay people the question,
'What or who was responsible for your coming to Christ
and your church?' Eight types of responses were generally given. Note which is most common.

1–2%: Special need
2–3%: Walk-in
5–6%: Pastor
1–2%: Visitation
4–5%: Sunday School
0.5%: Evangelistic Crusade
2–3%: Church Programme
75–95%: Friend/Relative[12]

3. Billy Graham's successful Seattle crusade in 1976 saw 18,136 persons come forward onto the astroturf to make commitments to Christ. Not all of these were incorporated into local churches, but of those who were, over eight out of ten already had a friend or relative in that particular congregation. Only 17.2% of those who had no friend or relative in an existing congregation ended up joining one.[13]

What does this say to us? Surely it screams out 'relationship'? The friendship factor is the key to successful evangelism. It says that the gospel flows best along relationship lines. If there is limited relationship, there is limited evangelism.

The bridges of God

Donald McGavran, called by some the 'father of the church growth movement', wrote a famous little book called *The Bridges of God* which revolutionised mission thinking. McGavran, himself a missionary in India, advocated on the foreign mission field what our above statistics indicated on the home mission field—that relationship lines must not be ignored.

McGavran contended that missionaries ought to take much more seriously the social groupings—the network of relationships—of those they are trying to reach. These social groupings, these networks of relationships, provide a sense of identity and worth. They are the means whereby the traditions and the values of a people are passed down through the generations. They are what makes a tribe a tribe. Understandably then, they are fiercely guarded and valued by the tribe.

McGavran said that missionaries are too ready to extract converts from their people, to isolate them in missionary compounds. Little do they realise that in doing this they are actually thwarting their deepest desire—to see the whole people group (tribe, nation, etc) evangelised. By extracting their converts they are cutting all relationship links. They are destroying their bridges to the tribe, for these relationships are the 'bridges of God' over which the gospel was meant to flow. The lesson is: build bridges not walls.

McGavran's insight not only holds true for primitive tribal societies in the Third World, it also applies to the individualistic West of the twentieth century. A 'people movement'—with the gospel flowing along relationship lines—is exactly what happened in Nottingham around my friend John Goodfellow. John, already mentioned in a previous chapter, had been converted in Amsterdam. After several months spent there being built up in his faith, he returned to his home town of Nottingham where he needed to make restitution for his old life of thievery. Upon his return home he began to share his new faith with family and friends, who told other family and friends, who told their family and friends. Within a few months there were over sixty people, mostly unchurched, crammed into his living room praying, praising and studying the Bible every Tuesday night. This meeting was never formally advertised. There was no billboard outside (unlike one billboard I saw outside a derelict church announcing to all the world, 'This church is being converted.' Amen!), no tracting campaign to pull people in. People came because of relationship links. The gospel spread along relationship lines. It was a question of one person, excited about what God had done in his life, sharing it with people he knew, ie friends and relatives. It was a loose-knit 'people movement'.

This is the missing element in much of our evangelism. Some years ago I was involved in a mission with a very lively church near Worthing in the south of England. The net sum of converts after an intense week of evangelistic meetings was zero. What went wrong? My analysis is this: the anointing was there, the effort was there, the gifts were there, the Holy Spirit was there, the church was there but—one shortcoming—the non-Christians weren't there! The mission was not build on a pre-existing base of relationships with non-Christians. There was no way they were going to enter a strange building holding strange religious activities with strange people. It's friendships which ease people past the 'stained-glass' barrier.

The early church did not ignore these bridges of relationship. Five of the twelve apostles had friendship/kinship links even before Jesus chose them. Peter and Andrew were brothers from the same small town of Bethsaida as Philip (Jn 1:44). James and John were Peter's business partners (Lk 5:10).

The apostle Paul, in spreading the gospel throughout the Mediterranean world, used the natural openings provided by relationship ties. Why was it that Paul, who said that his specific role was 'apostle to the Gentiles' (Gal 2:8), used to go first to the Jewish synagogue in each place he visited (see Acts 17:2)? I am convinced it was because he knew that the best way to reach the Gentiles was to use the bridge of relationships. He only went with 'cold contact' evangelism when he had to.

As a Jew, Paul had an immediate hearing in the synagogues. In Pisidian Antioch, for example, he did not even need to take the initiative to preach; they asked him if he had a message for them (Acts 13:15). Did he ever! But his natural openings did not stop there. Each synagogue was composed of three groups: Jews of the Hebrew race, Jews of the Greek/Gentile race (converts) and a fringe of believing but uncircumcised Greeks. It was these Gentiles who were Paul's bridge to the rest of the Gentile community. All of them had friends and relatives they could share with themselves or bring to hear Paul.

Acts 13 shows this friendship bridge strategy at work. First Paul goes to the synagogue to preach (vv 14–15). As a result 'many of the Jews and devout converts to Judaism followed Paul and Barnabas' (v 43). During the course of the ensuing week these Gentile converts must have told their Gentile friends and relatives about Paul's amazing story, because the next week, without any advertising or pushing by Paul, 'almost the whole city gathered to hear the word of the Lord' (v 44). Paul had reached the entire town just by going to the synagogue! Paul had lit the fuse, and the Holy Spirit, working down the relationship networks, had done the rest.

Radical separation and radical identification

Building bridges should be our aim in evangelism. But some of our Christian theology is more apt to build walls than bridges. A classic example is our emphasis on 'come out and be ye separate'. A wrong concept of 'separation from the world' will more effectively build walls than anything else. If it is central to our concept of the religious life that we should not drink, smoke, play cards, read novels, go to films or be with people who do, then we are in the wall-constructing business. Wall building is the occupational hazard of the religious person.

If we tell young converts they must sever all relationships with non-Christians, we are building walls. If we tell our congregations they must not do what non-Christians do—meaning cultural/social pursuits rather than sinful pursuits—we are building walls.

Relationships are built on common interests. No common interests—no relationships. You cannot just walk up to somebody saying, 'I want to be your friend,' and then stand there staring meaningfully into their eyes. No, you go out and play a game of squash (though maybe that would start a war, not a friendship) or go to see a film. You share an activity. But what can we do together with non-Christians if we have cut all unspiritual activities out of our lives? We can hardly expect non-Christians to share our church interests. It's hard enough trying to drag Christians along to the mid-week prayer meeting! An invitation to 'come along to our Bible study' scarcely sizzles with excitement for the unbeliever with his nose deep in Harold Robbins.

If non-Christians have no interests in common with Christians (church, Bible reading, prayer meetings, etc) and Christians have no interests in common with non-Christians (sport, work, hobbies, politics, etc) then never the twain shall meet. Christians end up walled off from the community around them, and you cannot do evangelism from behind walls.

The early church grew because it was not walled off from its surrounding community. It was ordinary Christians staying in contact with unbelievers through 'secular' involvements that was the channel through which the good news flowed. Church historian Kenneth Latourette writes, 'The chief agents in the expansion of Christianity appear not to have been those who made it a profession or a major part of their occupation, but men and women who earned their livelihood in some purely secular manner and spoke of their faith to those they met in this natural fashion.'[14]

Jesus did not come to earth to build a cosy little church with nice high walls keeping the big, bad world out. The heart of the Incarnation is God building a bridge from heaven to earth. There was no one in Palestine less walled off from people than Jesus of Nazareth. Wall-to-wall people, not walled off from people, would be the way to describe Jesus' ministry.

It was the Pharisees who were walled off from the community at large. They did not see their task, as one definition of evangelism has it, as 'one beggar offering another beggar bread'. They saw their chief task as keeping clean and keeping separate from sinful people. FF Bruce suggests that the central meaning of the word 'Pharisee' is 'separate'. He writes, 'It is...likely that they were called "Pharisees" in the sense of "separatists" because of their strict avoidance of everything which might convey ceremonial impurity to them.'[15]

Rebecca Manley Pippert writes of one

> very orthodox sect of the Pharisees called the "Bruised and Bleeding" Pharisees (who) thought lust was evil. So they determined they would avoid the source of the problem—namely, women. And whenever they came into the presence of a woman, not only would they avoid talking to her, they would close their eyes so that they could not see her at all. Of course this caused them to run into walls, and hence their name. Can you imagine the shock of an exceedingly pious member of the "Bruised and Bleeding" sect walking by and discovering Jesus deeply engaged in conversation with a prostitute?[16]

The Pharisees had a type of spirituality that made them inhuman. It separated them from people. Not so Jesus. Jesus was unconcerned for the externals of religious behaviour. Jesus was not bothered with always being seen to be spiritual. His spirituality did not consist of acting peculiar but in knowing God. He knew his God and got on with the business of mixing in down-to-earth ways with God's creatures. Rather than hiding away in a cave with incense and scrolls he walked the dusty roads. Not for him all this fussing with ceremonial washings and ritual bowings and scrapings. No, he went to festive banquets, mixed with the crowds, let the wine flow and enjoyed the hospitality of people's homes.

This was why one of the Pharisees' basic complaints against Jesus was, 'He's not religious enough.' 'The Son of Man came eating and drinking and you say, "Here is a glutton and a drunkard, a friend of tax collectors and 'sinners' " ' (Lk 7:34).

The Pharisees majored on minors; always a tragic waste of time. It has been well said that

> Legalism is making relatives absolute.
> Liberalism is making absolutes relative.

Jesus steered between both these extremes.

In the words of Mrs Pippert, we need to reclaim Jesus' sense of 'radical separation and radical identification'. On the outside the Pharisees were separate from the world, but on the inside they had the same values—love of money and position, pride, hatred. On the outside Jesus seemed the same as the world—he was an ordinary man with an ordinary profession (carpentry), wearing ordinary clothes—but on ultimate concerns, the things that really mattered to God, he was radically different.

Jesus was radically different in his holy, Spirit-led and Spirit-empowered lifestyle. But Jesus was also radically identified with the human race. Nothing could have been a greater step of identification than for God to become man.

If we lose our radical difference we have nothing to offer the world; we become unsalty salt, useless to God and man. And if we lose our radical identification we have no way of offering what we do have.

Identification means seeing where we can agree with non-Christians and mucking in at these points. It means, on all but crucial points, not trumpeting our differences. If, when an unbeliever lights up a fag in our living room, we straighten indignantly, arch our eyebrows and say, 'We don't smoke in our house. We're *Christians,*' (heavy emphasis on the last word) we are on a loser. Our calling is not primarily to be awkward. Faithfulness in evangelism is not measured by how uncomfortable our listeners are.

Identification means emphasising what we do rather than what we don't do. The don'ts are invariably what our non-Christian friends do! Producing a long shopping list of don'ts is not in Dale Carnegie's book on how to win friends and influence people, and it is not in God's either. One tribe in Zambia was completely indifferent to the gospel because they understood that its chief contribution to their lifestyle was to prevent them from drinking beer and marrying more than one wife.[17] In hearing mainly don'ts they were not hearing good news but bad news. But it is the good news which will win men and women to Christ.

We need to be both radically separate and radically identified; separate from sin but identified with people's humanity. Hudson Taylor, as a young missionary in China, found that to be effective in evangelism he not only had to mind spiritual realities but mundane, earthly realities. For instance, he found he could obtain a much better hearing if he wore native garb and donned the native hair piece, a long braid, than when he wore Western garb. One might think that a mighty spiritual anointing would do away with this sort of consideration, but evidently not. Taylor found that clothed like this he got an even better hearing than the experienced missionary, William Burns, who kept to Western attire. Burns was no spiritual slouch—indeed he was a household name in Scotland where he had been powerfully used in revival— but his Western attire built a small wall between himself and his listeners.[18] Taylor, on the other hand, was trying to identify with his listeners; not just with their spiritual needs but with their humanity. By dressing in the manner they dressed he was showing respect for their culture and, by extension, for them as individuals. That builds bridges.

People are more than disembodied souls that need saving. They are human beings who need valuing. Identification means we get alongside people's humanity. It means we not only pray for people's eternity but we accept the way they look, act, talk and dress in the here and now.

Identification was the apostle Paul's subject in writing, 'To those under the law I became like one under the law...so as to win those under the law. To those not having the law I became like one not having the law' (1 Cor 9:20–21). He made a conscious effort to look, act, talk and dress like those he was evangelising in order to open up a way for the gospel. He did not regard the more superficial areas of life—people's social customs— as unfit for consideration compared to the more weighty matters of eternity and spiritual reality. People's spirituality could only be reached through their humanity.

Notice what it was in Acts 22:2 which won for Paul the Jews' initial interest and which turned a riotous mob into sympathetic listeners: 'When they heard him speak to them in Aramaic, they became very quiet.' Aramaic was the mother tongue of Judea. The Jews suddenly thought, 'Hold on, he's one of us.' A simple thing like speaking their language turned a key. It was the identification factor at work, soothing hostility and opening up the way for communication.

For Hudson Taylor's audience the issue was hair braids and Fu Manchu moustaches. What is it for us in the modern, Western world? It might be dress, it might be leisure activities, it might be business involvements. Probably more important than *what* we do is *how* we do it. Do we have a narrow, cribbed, sour attitude to life? Do we think the Devil controls all the nice things in the world and that if something is bitter it's 'probably good for us'? Or are we convinced that 'the earth is the Lord's and the fulness thereof' (Ps 24:1, KJV)? Do we reach out to people seeing past their sins to the fact that they are created in the image of God? Do we condemn people as sinful, keeping them at arm's distance, or do we love them? That is the crux of the matter.

More than a technique

The friendship factor in evangelism needs to be more than a technique, more than a soulless tool to share the gospel. It needs to come out of a genuine desire to bless people. Otherwise it will simply be manipulation. The story has been told of a lady who answered the knock on her door to find a man with a sad expression.

'I'm sorry to disturb you,' he said, 'but I'm collecting money for an unfortunate family in the neighbourhood. The husband is out of work, the kids are hungry, the utilities will soon be cut off and, worse, they're going to be kicked out of their flat if they don't pay the rent by this afternoon.'

'I'll be happy to help,' said the woman with great concern. 'But who are you?'

'I'm the landlord,' he replied.

Pseudo-concern won't do the trick. It's God's love or

nothing. When we mix the gospel message with the love of God flowing through our hearts what happens is this: 'In every way they will make the teaching about God our Saviour attractive' (Tit 2:10). That's attractive evangelism. That's biblical evangelism.

6

Miracles: Icing on the Cake or Meat and Potatoes?

I am afraid that we have reversed the apostolic injunction, 'Silver and gold have I none, but such as I have give I thee... Walk,' to a paler and anaemic version, reading, 'Silver and gold have I some, but what I haven't got I can't give you!'

In Romans 15:18–19 Paul gives us God's audio-visual: '...in leading the Gentiles to obey God by what I have said and done—by the power of signs and miracles, through the power of the Spirit.' Paul, in describing how he evangelised, notes three elements: what he said, what he did (lifestyle of love) and what God did in miracles. Note the mix: one part words to two parts visual. Evangelism is not only talking about God, it is demonstrating God.

In the previous chapter we saw the premium God puts on demonstrating his love. But this is only half of it. God is not only loving, he is powerful. In fact, God's uniqueness is not in his love, it's in his God-ness (uncaused, infinite, etc). We need to demonstrate both God's character (the fruits of the Spirit) and his power (the gifts of the Spirit). No giver appreciates his gifts being shelved, much less does God.

An unbelieving world has to be grabbed by the scruff of the neck and given a good miraculous shake till its apathetic teeth rattle. Only then will it begin to take God seriously. In 1 Corinthians 14 the apostle Paul is cooling down the tongues-speakers and encouraging more use of the gift of prophecy, his point being that 'if an unbeliever or someone who does not understand comes in while everybody is prophesying, he will be convinced by all that he is a sinner and will be judged by all, and the secrets of his heart will be laid bare. So he will fall down and worship God, exclaiming, "God is really among you!" ' (vv 24–25). This is what people want to know: whether God is among us. They do not want to know if we have a good philosophy. Miracles shows that he is among us. Prophecy, showing the secret thoughts that no man knows, shows that God is alive and stalking the earth.

Though miracles are vital to effective evangelism, they are no guarantee of conversion. They cannot force the proud heart to submit. Jesus performed many miracles and still many did not believe in him. But for those with ears to hear and eyes to see, the miracles were a clear sign of Jesus' divine origin. Miracles were not called 'signs' (Jn 20:30) for nothing. They were meant as road signs on the way. As a road sign is not an end in itself (you would miss the point if you stopped your car, gawked at the sign and, with admiring oohs and ahs, took photos of it from different angles, hoping to capture the perfect sign picture) so the miracles were not ends in themselves. People were meant to read them, to interpret what they were saying. They pointed to Jesus, saying, 'Here's God's Son.'

Miracles are not just icing on the cake—extra frills, chrome bumpers instead of the plain model—but the meat and potatoes of evangelism. Jesus, the Son of God himself, did not think perfect holiness, stunning wisdom and anointed preaching sufficient to do the task. He needed miracles, and so do we.

When Jesus said, 'Unless you people see miraculous signs and wonders, you will never believe' (Jn 4:48), he may have been bemoaning the fact, but he was not thereby refusing to do miracles. He was not saying that performing miracles would simply pander to their unbelief. This we know, because the very man he had verbally whiplashed in this manner is the very man, in the next breath, he tells, 'You may go. Your son will live' (v 50). Miraculous healing. The result? 'So he and all his household believed' (v 53).

Miracles were and are central to the ministry of Jesus Christ. If you cut out all the miraculous accounts in the New Testament you would be left with such stirring statements as, 'And Jesus walked.... And Jesus ate some fish.... And Jesus reclined.' The guts of the New Testament would be gone.

But it was not only Jesus who had a miraculous ministry. Jesus was hatching a conspiracy during his sojourn on earth, and this conspiracy's central plot was to get his followers doing what he had been doing. One day he turned upon his unsuspecting followers and, in reference to the mob of 5,000 hungry worshippers, said, 'You give them something to eat' (Mk 6:37). They hadn't reckoned on this! Up to this time miracles had been the Master's exclusive province. They had been content just to stand by as admiring onlookers. But Jesus' conspiracy was on—Operation Transformation—with the disciples cast as the victims.

The disciples utterly failed this first lesson. I am sure

we would have been no different. Where Jesus, looking at the vast crowd, said, 'They do not need to go away' (Mt 14:16), we would have said, 'They do not need to...eat! Fasting is good for the soul.' No one likes to launch out beyond their natural limits. But the bad news is this: that's God's plan for us. The good news is this: we can do it. But we first have to get rid of a self-concept which limits us to the natural.

Our self-concept

Do you consider yourself a 'natural' Christian? You don't think of yourself as one of those 'supernatural' types always looking for a miracle. Just not your style? Do you think of yourself as a spiritual lightweight when it comes to the miraculous? If someone came to you with a cold, would you send them to the healing line of the next John Wimber conference?

Most of us are insecure in our supernaturalism. We find it difficult to take ourselves seriously as supernatural people. 'Raise the dead? Why, I can hardly get over this cold!'

Here's a sobering thought: our concept of ourselves can limit what God can do through us. It limited Jesus. About his ministry in his home town we read, 'He could not do any miracles there, except lay his hands on a few sick people and heal them' (Mk 6:5; cf Mt 13:58). Why did those from Jesus' home town have such unbelief? The clue comes in their very words. They said, 'Isn't this the carpenter? Isn't this Mary's son and the brother of James, Joses, Judas and Simon? Aren't his sisters here with us?' They knew him too well in the natural to believe in him as supernatural. And that's our trouble too. We know ourselves too well in the natural to readily believe in our supernatural side—the Holy Spirit within us.

Not that what Jesus' home town folk were saying was untrue. He was all those things: carpenter, family member, ordinary local citizen. But he was more than that. It's just that those who had grown up with him could not see the 'more'. They could not see past their memories of the ordinary boy playing and the normal man working to see the Son of God. In exactly the same way we find it difficult to look past our human limitations to see the divine anointing upon us as Christians.

Special ministries?

But are the dramatically supernatural gifts of the Spirit, such as healing and words of knowledge, reserved only for the special few? Can the ordinary Christian—you and I—expect to see these gifts in operation in our lives?

The gifts are for all. The scriptural formula is that we are to be a 'Jack-of-all-trades, master of some'. Who does the apostle James say should pray for the healing of the sick? First he tells the church to have the elders pray for the sick man and then he goes on to tell the congregation to 'pray for each other so that you may be healed' (Jas 5:14, 16). Nowhere does he enjoin them to go and look for someone with the specialist gift of healing.[19] He assumes, first, that this is something any elder can do and, secondly, that it is something every Christian can do. Who does that leave out?

To think that because we have not been given a specialist ministry of healing we cannot therefore pray effectively for the sick is the equivalent of thinking we cannot witness to someone because we do not have the ministry of evangelism. Can you imagine someone, if approached by a non-Christian asking, 'Can you tell me the way to

God? I'm desperate to know him,' saying in return, 'I'm sorry, I would really like to help you, but I am not an evangelist. It's not my ministry. But in two years we are going to have a mission with a tent an' all and maybe you could come back then?' You may not be an evangelist, but you can still share Jesus with people. Likewise, you may not be a 'healer' or a prophet, but you can still pray for healing or get a word from God.

Disadvantaged Christians?

Now it may come as a shock to us to discover that, in regard to the miraculous, Jesus had no more advantages than us. Do you really believe this? Perhaps we know this as theory, but it still has not sunk in. As the saying goes, 'The longest eight inches in the world is the eight inches between our heads and our hearts.' Jesus had no more natural ability to do miracles than we do. Jesus did not perform signs and wonders by virtue of being the second person of the Godhead. Jesus did miracles as a man stripped of his divinity. He did signs and wonders by the power of the Spirit of God within him; the same Holy Spirit that we have.

Jesus said, 'I tell you the truth, the Son can do nothing by himself' (Jn 5:19). Was he using a bit of preacher's license here? Speaker's hyperbole, to make a point? Evang-elastic-ally speaking? To make it perfectly clear that Jesus meant exactly what he said, he prefaced his statements with, 'I tell you the truth.' I think that means he was telling the truth.

Luke tells us that 'Jesus returned to Galilee in the power of the Spirit, and news about him spread through the whole countryside' (Lk 4:14). Jesus did not begin his supernatural ministry until he had been anointed with the Holy Spirit because it was by the Spirit's power that he performed these miracles. Only then did he make a splash in Galilee.

We read in Acts 2:22, 'Jesus of Nazareth was a man accredited by God to you by miracles, wonders and signs, which God did among you through him.' Jesus had an MA, a miracle accreditation. Note the wording: God doing it through Jesus. God did the miracles, not Jesus. In the Incarnation, Jesus set aside his divine power and became a man with human limitations. The miracles he did were done as a man trusting his Father in heaven, exactly as we have to do.

Lastly, we can usefully look at Acts 10:37–38 which says, 'You know... how God anointed Jesus of Nazareth with the Holy Spirit and power, and how he went around doing good and healing all who were under the power of the devil, because God was with him.' Once again, we see that Jesus' supernatural ministry was based not on his own power, but on his anointing by the Holy Spirit. He did not do miracles out of his own resources, but 'because God was with him'.

Easy-peasy

When I say, 'Four easy steps to a miracle,' I am, obviously, being somewhat cheeky; but not entirely. Performing miracles is easy on three counts.

First, because it is God who works the miracles, not our efforts. We cannot sweat our way into a miracle. Working hard at it is not the key. I can imagine an earnest, zealous, budding miracle-worker crying out, 'Oh, Lord, I've been on a complete fast now for four months and I finally feel the glory!' only to hear the Lord laconically reply, 'Yes, no doubt, because you are in glory. You have to eat, you idiot.'

Secondly, it is easy because you do not need a degree

in miracle-working to see a miracle. You do not need to go off for three years of Bible school, swotting up till the small hours of the morning. Intellectual equipment is not the key.

Thirdly, it is easy in the sense that the standard of holiness is not too high. Far and away the most popular misconception we Christians have concerning the supernatural is that only when we get ourselves a whole lot holier will God be able to start using us in the miraculous. Only when we attain that higher standard—a standard that is always just another sin away—can we trust that God will consent to work through us to see a sniffle stopped.

But consider the twelve apostles. Were they exceptionally deep, holy, wise, spiritual exemplars and pillars of Christian virtue? No, they loved Jesus, but they had all the failings we are all too familiar with. At such a delicate moment as the Last Supper, a poignant scene with Jesus giving his last goodbyes, the mood of high spirituality is ruined by the disciples' spirited argument 'as to which of them was considered to be greatest' (Lk 22:24). Selfish ambition rears its ugly head on the eve of the greatest act of self-sacrifice this world has ever known. Did this mean God could not use them to do great things? Not in the least.

Erlo Stegen was once relating to a group of us the marvellous revival that was taking place in South Africa, a revival sweeping multiplied thousands of Zulus into the kingdom. A friend of mine asked him who God was using, assuming that God would use the mature and sanctified Christians more than the immature ones. Great was his surprise when Erlo said, 'It doesn't matter. God is using everybody equally, mature and immature alike.'

How high is the standard of holiness required to do

miracles? Well, think of Jesus' words in Matthew 7:22–23: 'Many will say to me on that day, "Lord, Lord, did we not prophesy in your name, and in your name drive out demons and perform many miracles?" Then I will tell them plainly, "I never knew you. Away from me, you evildoers!" ' The question really ought to be, 'How *low* is the standard of holiness required?' The people Jesus was referring to had not even been saved! Yet still they were doing miracles.

Our holiness is not the key to the miraculous. God is the key to the miraculous. Peter said to the crowd gaping after his latest miracle, 'Men of Israel, why does this surprise you? Why do you stare at us as if by our own power or godliness we had made this man walk?' (Acts 3:12). We are all convinced that our own power is useless for a miracle. We are less convinced the same is true for our godliness. Don't wait to be perfect and holy before starting to attempt to walk in the supernatural. You will never get started. Perfection will always elude us this side of paradise, but miracles don't have to.

In this chapter we have been laying a foundation—showing the centrality of the miraculous to evangelism and dealing with those misconceptions which stop us from experiencing miracles. Having laid a foundation, let's begin to build. In the next chapter we shall go on to look at how we can actually introduce the miraculous into our experience. We don't want to meditate on miracles, we want to do them.

7

How to Do a Miracle
in Four Easy Steps

I had just been to a fantastic three-day conference on 'Signs and Wonders' by John Wimber, and was greatly challenged. I was also not a little frustrated. I wondered if there might not be more helpful advice on entering into the miraculous than the simple admonition to 'watch what the Father was doing and do that'. What if you couldn't see what the Father was doing? What if your eyesight was impaired through fear, unbelief or simple lack of practice? Were there any more concrete and specific steps one could take to walk into a miracle? Practising non-mystics like myself would find this most helpful. A goal without 'how-to' steps is a tantalising exercise in frustration. To put it quaintly: giving ends without means is mean.

When the Lord taught the disciples to pray (see Matthew 6:9ff), he did not leave them with vague, if deep, spiritual principles; principles they were unsure how to apply; principles that left them meditative but, frankly, confused. Jesus gave them some very practical 'how to's'. So concrete was he that he not only told them *how* to pray but *what* to pray. 'Copy me' was his method. I imagine their conversation went something like this:

'Just say after me, "Our Father...." '

'Our Father....'

'That's right; you're doing well. A little more clearly, please.'

'Our Father....'

'Better. Now say, "Who art in heaven." '

'Who's Art?'

'Never mind, just say it. Come on, let's get learning.' And on they went.

It was by copying Jesus that they learned to pray, and it was by copying Jesus that they learned to do miracles. That's what that rascal did who so irritated the disciples in Mark 9:38: ' "Teacher," said John, "we saw a man driving out demons in your name and we told him to stop, because he was not one of us." ' Three things are clear about this fellow: he believed in Jesus; he was doing miracles; his actual involvement with Jesus was minimal. The fact that the disciples, who were with Jesus constantly, had never seen him before means that either he had only met Jesus fleetingly or that he had simply watched Jesus minister from the edge of a crowd.

The question is: How did he, who obviously had never had sufficient time with Jesus to get any in-depth lessons, do miracles? I think he simply copied Jesus. I think that when he came across needy people he just did what he had seen the Teacher do. He would tentatively reach out his hand, as he had seen the Master do, and rebuke the spirit, as he had seen the Master do, in Jesus' name. He probably fell over in astonishment the first time it worked! The next time, his boldness growing, he would approach a blind man and, as he had seen the Teacher doing, spit in his eye—desperately thinking, 'There's going to be trouble if this doesn't work'—and pray.

It really must have been that simple. Certain it is that Jesus did not have a reserve squad—with this fellow being a member—that he was secretly training in case the first team fell through. And we can be quite convinced that this fellow hadn't gone down to the local bookstore to digest Jesus' latest bestseller, *Miracles and How I Work Them*.

We, too, want to walk in the footsteps of Jesus. We, too, want to copy what he did. While miracles are worked through faith (see Galatians 3:5) they are still worked. There is something we must do. James 2:22 says, 'His faith was made complete by what he did.' Real faith will be rooted in action. Read on to find out what sort of action this faith requires.

Jesus and Peter walk on water

In Matthew 14:22–36 the story is recounted of Jesus walking on water. But for us Christians this is almost old hat. We may read that Jesus had all the human limitations that we have, but still at gut level we can't help feeling that he cheated; that as the Son of God of course he raised the dead, healed the blind and, oh yes, walked on water.

What is truly amazing to us is that Peter also walked on water. Peter, an ordinary man with failings and foibles just like us. Now this is surprising. This was not natural! Water-walking was not an old family tradition that had been handed down through the centuries. It wasn't a common Galilean technique, perfected through much trial and error, to attract fish. History gives no record of any proverb circulating about Judea stating, 'Galileans are more buoyant!' No, this was unusual. This had never been done before. How did Peter do it? He did four key things. Here they are:

1. He put himself in a situation where God wanted to help

Peter only saw a miracle because he was with Jesus. If, instead of being out on the boat, he had been back home reading the *Jerusalem Gazette* with his knees up before the fire, he never would have seen this miracle. Who needs to walk on water when they are on their backside? It was only because Peter was up and following Jesus that he got himself into a situation where he needed to see a miracle.

What did Jesus mean, anyway, when he said to his disciples, 'Come and follow me'? It was not the metaphorical 'follow' we do today, but a literal, physical following. If Matthew had not literally come out from behind his tax table and followed Jesus he would have been rebuked. Following in his heart was not good enough.

Now Jesus did not tell them to follow because he was mad keen on them taking a Holy Land tour with him. And I am sure he did not think there was any virtue to be imbibed by queuing up behind him inhaling holy dust as it arose from his sacred sandals. No, he wanted them to be with him to join him in what he was doing, ie he wanted them to minister with him. He wanted the disciples to reach out and serve people as *he* was serving people. That was the real point.

If we want to see more of the miraculous in our lives, we must follow Jesus by getting out and serving people. The gifts of the Spirit are tools, not toys. You only need tools when you are doing some practical work. Tools are generally greasy and universally unattractive. That is why they are useless as decoration and are best hidden away until you are ready to do some real work. So it is with the gifts of the Holy Spirit.

Gifts of the Spirit are not for show but for practical use. King Herod was excited about having Jesus ushered into his court because, 'From what he had heard about him, he hoped to see him perform some miracle' (Lk 23:8). But Jesus did nothing. Why? Because Herod wanted 'to see him perform'. Jesus was not there to perform. He only did miracles when they served a real need.

Upon returning from the above-mentioned John Wimber 'Signs and Wonders' conference I got together with my prayer group and we began to implore the Lord to show his power among us. After five minutes of fervent pleading I began to feel that our behaviour was more than slightly ridiculous. It seemed to me that the Lord was calmly listening to our impassioned requests and quietly responding, 'Yes,' each time we asked. No amount of fervent prayer could improve on that answer. We had what we were asking for, but now what?

I suggested to our group that it would be far better to pray for one another's real needs by simply believing that the Lord would give us whatever miraculous tool was necessary for the situation. That's just what we did, the upshot being that two people who had never received words of knowledge before were given some by the Lord. The girl we were praying for ended up weeping with joy, so deep was the ministry she received from these words of knowledge. All this had happened because we had put ourselves in a situation where God would want to help us; we had been reaching out to serve people.

God's power is more like the electricity buzzing around your wiring which just needs a switch to flick it on. The switch is service. The power is always there.

Unlike a reservoir that needs refilling, electricity is always there. It's ready when you are.

A friend of mine periodically complains, 'God never speaks to me.' However, whenever she is urged to team up with my wife to counsel someone she invariably gets words of wisdom and knowledge bringing help and insight. Though she does not feel herself to be a spiritual dynamo, once she flicks on the switch of service, God comes through every time. If you don't flick the switch, the electricity will not come on. If you don't reach out to serve people, you will never see God's miraculous power work through you.

2. *He had the desire*

Who initiated the miracle in Matthew 14, Jesus or Peter? Do we see Jesus yelling through the storm, 'Who's got guts enough to come to me? First one out is chief disciple; last one out is a rotten egg.' Not a bit of it. Peter initiated this miraculous event by asking, 'Lord, I'd like to do that. Can I? If it's you, tell me to come to you on the water.'

In 1 Corinthians 14:1, Paul tells the Corinthians to 'eagerly desire spiritual gifts, especially the gift of prophecy'. Now this is a curious thing. Isn't the manifestation of the gifts totally up to God in his sovereignty? But Paul would hardly be telling them to desire gifts if human desire was totally irrelevant. The biblical approach is that 'God...works in you to will and to act according to his good purpose' (Phil 2:13). Acting comes out of first willing. God does not want to coerce us; he wants to co-operate with us. We are God's co-workers (1 Cor 3:9). Our desires are relevant. If we do not want to see a miracle, chances are we won't.

But really, would any Christian not want to see a miracle? The answer to that is yes, especially once it becomes clear that miracles don't happen on the side-lines but occur as you and I step out on a limb. Stepping out on a limb can be dangerous. We might fall off.

Fear kills desire. Fear reminds us of past mistakes. Fear focuses on what might go wrong, the embarrassment we might suffer. Fear is like one of those accident signs one sees at dangerous corners in London blasting out, 'DANGER, 4 people killed at this corner last weekend.' Immediately one brakes and proceeds with caution. If Peter had moved with caution he never would have moved. Fear kills.

Unbelief also kills desire. Indeed, unbelief is the source of fear. The moment a desire arises for a miracle, doubt comes in to strangle it saying, 'Who do you think you are kidding? God does not do that sort of thing through you.' Unbelief makes the miraculous seem weird instead of God-natural. The supernatural is not weird, it's natural...to God. But unbelief whispers to us that we are reverting to the superstitious Middle Ages. Why, next we'll be burning witches!

The Western world is in the grasp of a rationalism that discounts God and all of the supernatural. Naturalism— all things having natural causes and explanations—is the ruling prejudice of the day. But it must be overruled. Paul's no-nonsense approach was, 'We demolish arguments and every pretension that sets itself up against the knowledge of God' (2 Cor 10;5). Demolish it. Refuse to be ruled by this non-Christian philosophy. Don't doubt God; doubt your doubts.

Rationalism, not rationality, is anti-Christian. Rationality is simply logical thinking, using the brain God gave us. Nothing wrong with that. God did not give us a brain simply as ballast to hold down our necks. Rationalism, however, I define as that belief which places man's reason in an autonomous position from God, saying that it alone is a reliable guide to truth.

Rationalism is not only a thought-form to be rejected but a spirit to be renounced. Bill Subritzky, senior partner in a large law firm and governing director of one of New Zealand's largest homebuilding companies, tells the following story.

> On one occasion I was ministering with a well-known churchman when he remarked that he had never sensed the anointing of God. I suggested that he might have a mind block, which can arise as a result of training which questions the credibility of the Bible.
>
> A very humble man, he readily agreed to my suggestion that he renounce this spirit of blockage of mind. As he did so in the name of Jesus, the anointing of God came upon him and he gently fell to the floor, slain under the power of the Holy Spirit. He has known the reality of the anointing ever since.[20]

When seeking God for a miraculous gift of the Holy Spirit it would be no bad thing to renounce the spirit of rationalism that soaks that Western world. It is peculiar to us. See, by contrast, the Eastern world. A Channel Four reporter doing a special on the spiritist healers of Indonesia was amazed when, in the course of his filming, he himself was healed of an eye disease. His scepticism banished, the reporter ended the programme with a shot of this healer setting fire to a newspaper solely with the spiritual heat from his hand while a portentous voice-over said, 'What do these people living in the shadow of the volcano know that we of the West have forgotten?' The East believes in the supernatural—even if it fails to discern the satanic from the godly.

We Westerners need to renounce this spirit of rationalism saying, 'In Jesus' name I renounce this spirit.

I stand on the blood of Jesus and refuse to be dominated by this spirit of unbelief. Lord I submit my mind to you believing that "we have the mind of Christ" (1 Cor 2:16). For you, miracles are supernaturally natural.' Having done this we will be freer to desire that which God desires.

Desire is important. Without a strong desire, our good intentions flicker out and die; they are washed into oblivion by the tides of adversity. Management consultant Peter Drucker, after studying hundreds of successful businesses, concluded, 'Whenever anything is being accomplished, it is being done, I have learned, by a monomaniac with a mission.'[21] Monomaniac with a mission! Is this just a useless, secular insight? No, I think this is one of those insights of which Jesus said, 'The people of this world are more shrewd in dealing with their own kind than are the people of the light' (Lk 16:8). It is people with fixed and firm desires that get things done, whether those things be natural or supernatural.

Nourish this desire. Meditate on the promises of God and on the ministry of Jesus. Dare to believe that he wants to work through your life.

3. He stepped out beyond his own limits

In Matthew 14 Peter not only was busy following Jesus; not only was he desiring to see a miracle, he also— here's step three—literally put feet to his desire. He stepped out of the boat. Desire is an important initial step, but it alone is not the key to miracles. We need to do something as well. Remember James 2:17, 'Faith by itself, if it is not accompanied by action, is dead.' Dead faith is not much good to anyone. After a while it begins to stink.

Peter let God into his situation by stepping out beyond his own limits. Until we step out beyond our own limits we really do not need God's power. We are doing fine on our own, thank you very much.

A W Tozer once wrote, 'In the missionary society with which I have for many years been associated I have noticed that the power of God has always hovered over our frontiers. Miracles have accompanied our advances and have ceased when and where we allowed ourselves to become satisfied and ceased to advance.'[22] Are we pushing out into new frontiers? Maybe that's why we do not see more miracles. I think it is. I think rather than waiting and hoping that God will 'sovereignly' pour out the Spirit of miracles we should be stepping out into new challenges for God. Man is waiting for God, but God is waiting for man!

As the initiative with the desiring was with Peter so the initiative with the stepping out was with Peter. True, he avoided presumption by first asking Jesus, 'Lord, if it's you, tell me to come to you.' He waited on a word from Jesus. But once Jesus had answered, it was all over to Peter.

No celestial chariot broke the threatening clouds, swooping down and lifting him out of the boat to deposit him regally on the water. No myriads of angels in attentance lustily singing Handel's Hallelujah Chorus to encourage him. Just Jesus, Peter and the storm.

All Peter had was that little word, 'Come' (Mt 14:29). Can't you just imagine Peter kicking himself for his brashness and wondering, 'What's the Greek root of that word "come"? I wonder what Jesus could mean by that?' Meanwhile, the other disciples would be elbowing one another, enjoying Peter's predicament and waiting to see what he would do next. 'Peter's really done it this time. He's gone off at the deep end...or will do in a minute.'

Now Peter begins to step out of the boat. No divine help yet. One foot overboard; still no sign of divine help.

Toes dangling in the water now—Peter thinking, 'Yep, that water feels as wet and as sinkable as I remember.' Both feet over the side of the boat and *still* no sign of a miracle. Finally, as the disciples rise to their feet thinking, 'Oh no, the fool is actually going to do it,' Peter lets go and flings himself away from the boat. He finds he is walking on water! *Now* God steps in with a miracle.

Peter only needed God's miraculous intervention once he had let go of the boat. Up till then he could make it on his own. Remember, Peter did not have a special water-walking ministry. The only difference between Peter and the other disciples was that he let God into the situation by stepping out beyond his own limits.

Perhaps the next morning the disciples sat around the breakfast campfire, grumbling, 'Why don't we see more walking on water around here?' (Have you ever been part of a conversation like that? I have.) Peter would simply reply, 'How many times have you tried?' How many times have *you* tried?

I shall always remember John Wimber saying, 'I walked into a pastor's conference and asked how many of them had seen more than a handful healed through their prayers in the past year. Nobody raised their hand. Then I asked how many had prayed for more than a handful. Nobody raised their hand. Then I said that I had seen approximately two hundred people healed through my prayers. Impressive? I then pointed out that I had prayed for about six hundred people. I had failed more than I had succeeded.' But the point is that two hundred people had been helped, who would not have been, because he was trying, albeit imperfectly.

We have to give God time and place. He does not always make it easy for us. He wants us to be like Peter who took the initiative, who took steps that were too big for himself in the natural. Think of other miracles where the same principle was at work. In catching the miraculous load of fish, after toiling unsuccessfully all night they had to row right back out and let their nets down. Only after they did this—at the risk of looking idiots— did the miracle occur (see Luke 5). With the feeding of the five thousand the disciples first had to circulate through the crowd divvying up two fish and five loaves, already divided twelve ways! Only then did the miracle take place; not while they were sitting and praying over the supplies, peeping through their clasped hands, desperately looking for even the least hint of multiplication before they had to go out to the multitudes.

It's no use hanging about inside the boat. We need to give God time and place by stepping out of the boat. One of my first words of knowledge came in exactly this fashion. I had been meditating on this passage in Matthew 14 and, in fact, was going to be speaking on it that very evening at a Youth With A Mission celebration. I thought, 'There's no way I can speak on "How to do a miracle in four easy steps" and escape applying it myself.' So I said to the Lord, 'Lord, I would like a word of knowledge.' Now if you are perceptive and have been paying attention to what I have said up till now, you will notice that I had just applied my first two steps: I had put myself in a serving situation and had desired a miracle.

I then prayed against a spirit of unbelief and simply waited on the Lord for what he would say. There followed whatever follows when we wait on the Lord: 'Pizza...Sunday dinner...Good game on Saturday....' A jumble of disjointed, unspiritual thoughts that rotated around the week and back again, only momentarily seeming to touch on what I was wanting to pray about— God, the Bible and other more exalted subjects. But on I pressed. After no more than ten minutes of this I decided enough was enough. I must say that along with pizza and Saturday football one other thought had stood out to me. It was, 'A forty-three-year-old woman undergoing hassles at her church.' This thought had not come over with any more spiritual vibrations than had 'pizza'. Of course, it could have been a dual word; pizza and spiritual hassles, or spiritual hassles because of no pizza. In the end I dropped the pizza and ran with 'spiritual hassles'.

At the end of my message that night I looked out over the congregation and, seeing mainly young faces, muttered, 'Lord, the odds don't look too good here tonight.' But I knew I would kick myself for the rest of my life if I did not give this word. I could not have lived with for ever wondering if 'that word I had back in 1984 about a forty-three-year-old lady really was from the Lord'. I quickly weighed up how I might step out while affording myself maximum protection from embarrassment should I prove to be wrong. I thought I saw a way.

I ponderously said, 'And let us all rise, bow our heads, close our eyes and finish in prayer.' At this point I sneaked in a rapid fire, all in one breath, 'And-if-there-is-anyone-out-there-who-is-a-forty-three-year-old-lady-undergoing-church-hassles-please-come-up-and-see-me-for-prayer,' and then resumed a more stately, measured pace, closing with, 'And so we thank you for this evening. Amen. Let's sing number twenty-six in the songbook.' I had successfully sandwiched my bit as unobtrusively as possible between my usual closing prayers. Now I would just have to wait and see what happened.

It was with relief that I saw a lady approach me and sit down saying, 'Those were amazing details you got. They fit my situation exactly.' Hopping inside, I leaned back and dropped a casual, 'Oh sure.' God had come through!

God had done it, but he had required me to desire it and then to take a step. Sometimes one step is not enough. Sometimes we have to keep coming back to God, refusing to be put off by his initial lack of response. Surely this is the lesson of the Canaanite women in Matthew 15:21–28? Persistence is needed.

Bill Subritzky explains persistence was vital in his coming into the ministry of the word of knowledge. A Pentecostal brother who operated very freely in this gift took him under his wing.

> He would have a tremendous word for thirty, forty or fifty people as he stood with them towards the end of the meeting. As I stood next to him, he would ask, "Brother Bill, do you hear anything from the Lord?" I would say, "No, nothing."
>
> That happened the first week, the second week, the third week, the fourth week—thirty-five weeks in all. "Brother Bill, do you hear anything from the Lord?" I heard nothing!
>
> ...One night during the thirty-sixth week, as I hung in there, the anointing came upon me and something was impressed upon my mind. I began to speak out concerning the person before me. Within moments the brother said, "Bill, that's from the Lord—I have the same word!"[23]

Subritzky was only released in this gift as he pressed forward persistently in his desire to receive all that God wanted to give. Week after week he persisted. He did not let failure stop him. More than simply desiring, he stepped out of the boat by going down the prayer line ready for a word. He was not just lazing in the sovereignty of God. He put his faith to work. German theologian Helmut Thielecke once said, 'You can loaf your way into hell but the kingdom of heaven suffers violence, and the violent take it by force.'

God will not do it all for us. Man has a part to play. Of

course, this does not mean that we should begin to take credit for any of the miracles that are done through us. That would be as foolish as the woodpecker who, while he was ardently drilling for worms, had his tree knocked over by a mighty bolt of lightning. Unaware that lightning had struck, the woodpecker looked in amazement at the felled tree and began to preen himself thinking, 'What a mighty pecker I have that I should be able to knock down a tree.' Don't be stupid. God is the one who does the miracle.

Step out of the boat. Let God into your situation by getting out on a limb somewhere beyond your own abilities. It's risky but rewarding. Peter got wet, but he was the one who had the testimony that he had walked on water.

4. He exercised faith

There is no getting away from the fact that faith is the key to working miracles. It is faith that will move mountains (Mt 17:20), not love, hope, kindness or any other of the attractive Christian virtues. It was lack of faith that landed Peter in the lake—'Why did you doubt?' (Mt 14:31). Paul asks the Galatians, 'Does God give you his Spirit and work miracles among you because you observe the law, or because you believe what you heard?'—the obvious answer being it is because they believe. When the apostles asked Jesus why they could not cast a spirit out, Jesus told them point blank, 'Because you have so little faith' (Mt 17:20).

But what is this faith? How can we get it and how do we express it? Is faith 'believing what you know isn't true', as one young man put it, or, in the words of the cynic, 'the illogical belief in the improbable'? Is faith the great unobtainable object beyond the grasp of all but the most super-spiritual?

107

In finding our way forward, it is extremely helpful to differentiate the two kinds of faith we see in Scripture: will-do faith and can-do faith.

Will-do faith

Will-do faith is exemplified in the following accounts.

Matthew 9:21–22 recounts the story of the woman who had been subject to bleeding for twelve years. 'She said to herself, "If I only touch his cloak, I will be healed." Jesus turned and saw her. "Take heart, daughter," he said, "your faith has healed you." And the woman was healed from that moment.' The faith which she had was will-do faith. No questions, no doubts. The outcome was certain. She did not think, 'I might be healed,' but, 'I will be healed.' This faith moved the hand of God for healing.

Mark 11:22–24 portrays Jesus before the fruitless fig tree telling his disciples,

> Have faith in God. I tell you the truth, if anyone says to this mountain, "Go, throw yourself into the sea," and does not doubt in his heart but believes that what he says will happen, it will be done for him. Therefore I tell you, whatever you ask for in prayer, believe that you have received it, and it will be yours.

The type of faith Jesus is enjoining them to have is will-do faith. It's a faith that is certain of the outcome.

This is the sort of faith that moves God's hand in miracles. But this is also the type of faith that most of us find most difficult to operate. We wonder, for instance, when healing has been prayed for whether we should just believe we have been healed despite the symptoms that persist. Isn't that what Jesus is on about here in Mark 11?

My reply is twofold. First, we need to be listening to what the Lord tells us in the situation. This is just what Peter did when he was faced with his water-walking dilemma. He did not have a doctrine of water-walking, he had the Water-walker there to tell him specifically what to do. Ask what the Spirit is saying. Secondly, it seems that what Jesus is describing in Mark 11 is the 'gift of faith' (1 Cor 12:9). God just drops a certainty into our hearts that something is going to happen. We do not have to work it up, it's just there. When God drops this into our hearts we do not wonder whether we should believe for something, we know we should.

God, in his graciousness, not only works in response to will-do faith, he also responds to can-do faith.

Can-do faith

Matthew 9:27–29 shows Jesus meeting two blind men seeking healing. Jesus asked, ' "Do you believe that I am able to do this?" "Yes, Lord," they replied. Then he touched their eyes and said, "According to your faith will it be done to you;" and their sight was restored.' What sort of faith was it that released the miraculous? It was can-do faith. Jesus was fishing for this. Before he healed he wanted to make sure they were exercising it. Once he saw that, he was satisfied and he moved into action.

Notice that he did not say, 'I'm sorry. Can-do faith is only a starter. What I really want to know is whether you believe that once I touch your eyes they definitely will be healed. Until then there is not a lot I can do.' No, can-do faith suffices. Notice, too, that he also calls this can-do variety faith. It's not just hope, it's real faith. It may not be of the resilient will-do stock, but faith it is nevertheless. It moves the hand of God.

Mark 9:22–25 presents us with a pitiable scene: a distraught father bringing his beloved son, his only son (Lk 9:38), and imploring Jesus to free him from the cruel grasp of Satan. Year after year he had had to watch helplessly as Satan tormented his son. Now, for the first time in his life, he saw hope. He begged Jesus, ' "But if you can do anything, take pity on us and help us." "If you can?" said Jesus. "Everything is possible for him who believes." Immediately the boy's father exclaimed, "I do believe; help me overcome my unbelief!" When Jesus saw that a crowd was running to the scene, he rebuked the evil spirit.'

Jesus does not immediately heal the son. He stops and says, in effect, 'What's this "if you can" stuff? Stop right there. Before we proceed any further let's get this straightened out right here and now.' Immediately upon receiving this rebuke the boy's father decides he believes. Believes what? Why, that Jesus can do this healing. No more 'ifs'. It was can-do faith, and not necessarily of the most robust sort either. It's mixed with unbelief. He cries out, 'I do believe; help me overcome my unbelief!' But that's good enough for Jesus. He springs into action and the chains of years are released in a moment.

God will work through can-do faith if we will only exercise it.

Several years ago we had some New Zealanders staying with us at our London Discipleship House. John, a non-Christian doing his once-in-a-lifetime pilgrimage to the mother country (mandatory for any self-respecting New Zealander), had come to visit one of his friends at our house. We all went out for a picnic and found a nice cow field in which to play with a frisbee. Cow fields tend to have uneven surfaces and are full of land mines of one sort or another. John, after one particularly high leap, landed on one of these uneven surfaces and consequently badly twisted his ankle. I could see his face contort with pain from sixty feet away.

We rushed over to him, picked him up and gingerly moved him to the sidelines. It was clear he could play no more. I then thought, 'Lord, here's a need. Here's an opportunity to glorify your name. This is the type of situation where, in the New Testament, you would heal people. Why not now?' Why not indeed.

Note my attitude. It was, 'Why not?' rather than, 'Of course he will.' We told John we would like to pray for him and, as he couldn't go anywhere, he consented. Later he told us he was thinking, 'I wish these nuts would leave me alone.' But guess what—he was totally and instantly healed! A look of total bafflement coming over his face, he said, 'The pain's gone.' He stood up and warily tested it out. Yep, no more pain. So—what did we do? We just resumed our game.

You can imagine that we did not have to say much to John. God had evangelised him. He went back to our house, turning the miracle over and over in his mind, trying to explain it away. But every time he returned to the only plausible explanation: 'It was God.' Within a few days he had become a Christian.

The point is: it was can-do faith that worked this miracle, not will-do faith.

In 1980 my wife and I met a sixty-year-old lady from Chichester, the occasion for our brief encounter being a shared parking spot in Battle, south England. Within minutes we were in conversation and sharing our faith. Hearing that she was afflicted with asthma, we offered to pray for her. We were not convinced that she would be healed, but we were convinced that Jesus could heal her. Was 'could' enough though?

After quickly praying for her there on the spot—an

experience she found novel indeed, having scarcely prayed in church, much less a car park—we slipped her our address saying, 'If God heals you we'd love to hear about it.' You can see from the 'if' just where our faith was. But who cares where our faith was? God healed her.

In a letter she sent us two years later at Christmas—a letter which I treasure to this day—she wrote, 'I just recently found your address tucked in my wallet. You prayed for my health, and asked God to give me relief from the asthma that I suffer from. Well, do you know something? I have not had asthma for two years. Since I met you both that day in Battle I can honestly say that I have only got better.... Now isn't this just wonderful news?' She then added on a cute note which is actually spot-on theologically, 'I have likened you to "modern-day" disciples spreading the word of God.' We modern disciples are supposed to be like the New Testament disciples.

This woman had sought relief from asthma for twenty-one years. For twenty-one years she had taken steroids to combat the asthma, but to no avail. In fact, she had taken so many steroids that to her dangerous asthmatic condition was added the side-effect of painfully swollen joints. What medicine could not do, God did in response to two simple prayers; two can-do faith prayers.

Do not despise your can-do faith. Use what you have and God will give you more. As we exercise our faith by serving God, by desiring his miraculous intervention and by stepping out beyond our limits we will see God move. Our evangelism will become more like Jesus' evangelism. We will be able to say, like Paul, 'I will speak... of... what Christ has accomplished through me... by what I have said and done—by the power of signs and miracles, through the power of the Spirit.' And that can't be bad.

8

Open-Air Evangelism

'Kill, kill!' raged the infuriated man, launching himself at my neck.

This was no bad dream, but simply one day in the life of a street preacher. That Friday night I had taken a group of us down to London's Leicester Square which, since it is thronged with people at the weekends, is an excellent place for open airs. When we got down there we were disappointed to find the 'Budgie Man' already on our spot, entertaining the crowds with his pet dog and trained budgies.

Breathtaking hops through hoops and death-defying leaps through fires went on for a full forty-five minutes while our group of forty waited on the sidelines. I approached him during a break, saying we would like to go on next and could he finish soon please. He indicated that he would do no such thing and that, indeed, he intended to spend the entire evening on this nice little spot. Now that breaks the unwritten rule of the square among buskers, street preachers and other unsavouries.

If he indicated one thing, I indicated another: namely, that we would give him five more minutes after which we would set ourselves up just ten feet away to commence our programme of lusty singing. At this point, the atmosphere in our conversation was approaching warm-ish and I thought it best to take my leave.

As I was walking away I threw a remark over my shoulder, 'Remember, five more minutes,' punching the air with my open hand, my five fingers outstretched, to ensure he got the point. That was the last straw. He rushed over to me, his face contorted with hate and anger, and flung his arms around my neck in an effort to wrestle me to the ground. Fortunately, I had about five inches in height on him so that all I had to do to prevent myself being thrown was to wrap my arms around him, pull him in close and lift him up a little. There we grappled, his arms around me and mine around him—our struggle now looking less and less like the epic battle of the titans and more and more like a fervent hugging contest.

It was then, in frustration, that he yelled to his trained dog, 'Kill, kill!' The dog was just a little runt, one of those elongated hot dog types, so I was not too worried. But I did keep one eye open for him as Budgie Man and I spun about in our dance/hug routine, wondering if he had been specially trained in some sort of kamikaze technique; a secret weapon to clear away competing buskers. But he simply hovered nearby and yapped excitedly, his beady little eyes bearing down on me. Within two minutes the scene was over. Budgie Man got his five minutes and we got our open-air spot.

Open air's our heritage

Open-air preaching has always been a feature of Christian preaching. It is woven throughout the Bible. Jeremiah was sent by God to stand at the city gates to proclaim God's message to all the inhabitants of Jerusalem as they passed by (Jer 17:19). Jonah's commission was to range up and down the streets of the great city of Nineveh crying out, 'Forty more days and Nineveh will be destroyed' (Jon 3:4). The only thing he lacked was a sandwich board. Jesus' pulpit was often on a mountainside, off a seashore or in the city streets.

In the eighteenth-century revival which swept through Britain, open-air preaching was a chief feature. People who never darkened a church doorway would stop to hear a sermon in the open air. George Whitefield, famous eighteenth-century evangelist, first tried this revolutionary 'new' approach with the miners outside Bristol. Strangers seldom ventured into the miners' settlement, so notorious was it for viciousness. On occasion, seized by a wild mob spirit, the miners had stormed into Bristol, pillaging and terrorising until the crazed mood spent itself.

It was to these rough people that Whitefield went. His preaching touched hearts and soon he had crowds of up to ten thousand listening to him. He records his impressions:

Having no righteousness of their own to renounce, they were glad to hear of a Jesus who was a friend of publicans, and came not to call the righteous, but sinners to repentance. The first discovery of their being affected was to see the white gutters made by their tears which plentifully fell down their black cheeks, as they came out of their coal pits. Hundreds and hundreds of them, which, as the event

115

proved, happily ended in a sound and thorough conversion.[24]

Of course, open-air preaching was not always so well received. Jesus often, in his open-air preaching, stirred up a hornet's nest. Several times the crowd even attempted to kill him. If, as Jesus said, no one is greater than their master, we can expect the same. John Wesley, founder of Methodism, certainly found this. John, who was introduced to open-air preaching by Whitefield, kept a daily diary in which he related some of the opposition he faced in the course of his open-air meetings. These events outlined below are set in 1743 near Birmingham. A mob of two hundred had travelled through the night to bring him to trial for his 'crime' (preaching) when they were overtaken by another mob, equally hungry for blood. Forgive the longish quotation but I thought all of it too good to miss.

But we had not gone a hundred yards when the mob of Walsal came, pouring in like a flood, and bore down all before them. The Darlaston mob made what defence they could; but they were weary as well as outnumbered: so that in a short time, many being knocked down, the rest ran away and left me in their hands.

The poor woman of Darlaston, who had headed that mob...when she saw her followers give way, ran into the thickest of the throng and knocked down three or four men, one after another. But many assaulted her at once, she was soon overpowered and had probably been killed in a few minutes (three men keeping her down and beating her with all their might) had not a man called to one of them, "Hold, Tom, hold!" "Who is there?" said Tom: "What, honest Munchin'? Nay, then, let her go." So they held their hand and let her get up and crawl home as well as she could.

To attempt speaking was vain; for the noise on every side was like the roaring of the sea. So they dragged me along till

116

we came to the town; where seeing the door of a large house open, I attempted to go in; but a man, catching me by the hair, pulled me back into the middle of the mob. They made no more stop till they had carried me through the main street, from one end of the town to the other. I continued speaking all the time to those within hearing, feeling no pain or weariness. At the west end of the town, seeing a door half open, I made toward it and would have done, but a gentleman in the shop would not suffer me, saying they would pull the house down to the ground. However, I stood at the door, and asked, "Are you willing to hear me speak?" Many cried out, "No, no! knock his brains out; down with him; kill him at once." Others said, "Nay, but we will hear him first." I began asking, "What evil have I done? Which of you all have I wronged in word or deed?" And continued speaking for above a quarter of an hour, till my voice suddenly failed: then the floods began to lift up their voice again; many crying out, "Bring him away! bring him away!"

In the meantime my strength and my voice returned, and I broke out aloud in prayer. And now the man who just before headed the mob turned and said, "Sir, I will spend my life for you: follow me, and not one soul here shall touch a hair of your head." Two or three of his fellows confirmed his word and got close to me immediately. At the same time, the gentleman in the shop cried out, "For shame, for shame! Let him go."...God brought me safe to Wednesbury; I having lost only one flap of my waistcoat and a little skin from one of my hands.

The circumstances that follow, I thought, were particularly remarkable: 1) That many endeavoured to throw me down while we were going downhill on a slippery path to the town; as well judging, that if I was once on the ground, I should hardly rise any more.... 2) That a lusty man just behind struck at me several times with a large oaken stick, with which if he had struck me once on the back part of my head, it would have saved him all further trouble. But every time the blow was turned aside, I know not how; for I could not move to the right hand or left. 3) That another came rushing through the press and, raising his arm to strike, on a sudden let it drop and only stroked my head, saying, "What soft hair he has!" 4) That I stopped exactly at the mayor's door, as if I had known it (which the mob doubtless thought I did), and found him standing in the shop, his presence giving the first check to the madness of the people. 5) That the very first men whose hearts were turned were the heroes of the town, the captains of the rabble on all occasions, one of them having been a prizefighter at the bear-garden.[25]

John Wesley and his Methodists changed the face of England, and open-air preaching was their big gun, their first line of attack upon the immorality and unbelief of their age. The *Cambridge Modern History* says, 'For universality of influence he had no rival.'[26] By the time he died the number of Methodist members in the British dominions was 76,968, and in the United States was 57,621.[27] The Methodists' fervent open-air work conducted by unsophisticated preachers may not have been everywhere admired—one wag calling them 'illiterate mechanics, more fitted to make a pulpit than to get into one'—but they were effective everywhere.

Open-air preaching is part of our Christian heritage, a heritage that should be treasured.

Fresh air good for the soul

Open-air evangelism is good for you, good for others and bad for the Devil. Standing up for Jesus for the whole world to see invigorates our spirits. We are no longer meekly hiding away and minding our own business. We are sticking our heads out of our foxholes, going up and over and minding the Father's business. 'Look! The Hebrews are crawling out of the holes they were hiding in' (1 Sam 14:11) says the world in astonishment.

There is something in every Christian that thrills to

standing up for Jesus. We were made to be witnesses. Even the persecution that sometimes arises from this stand does not blunt this deep satisfaction; witness the disciples in Acts 5:41: 'The apostles left the Sanhedrin, rejoicing because they had been counted worthy of suffering disgrace for the Name.' There was joy in identifying with Jesus, whether in good times or bad times.

But open-air evangelism is not only good for you, it's good for others. It's a wonderful way to come in contact with strangers. It gets the gospel out to many who might not hear otherwise. It brings God to the attention of people who might never even think about him. Certainly some people are put off by open-air street meetings, but I would say for every response of, 'Shaddup, will yer,' I've had six, 'Well, I don't agree with what you're saying, but I admire your conviction in coming out and saying it.'

Jesus deserves to be proclaimed in the streets. He is the Lord of all the earth, the marketplaces and the high roads as well as the prayer closets and quiet sanctuaries. He is Lord, and the world needs to know about it. There can be few thrills to match an open air meeting where forty to eighty people crowd around intently listening, drinking in the word of God. Many a time it has been this crowd, not the Christians, who have impatiently silenced a heckler, saying they want to listen.

Open-air evangelism is good for spiritual warfare. The Devil hates to hear the name of Jesus proclaimed. It weakens his grip. Where the Devil would say, 'Aha, this is mine' (free rendering of Ezekiel 36:2), in reference to our towns and cities, we can say they belong to God.

Open-air evangelism is not the whole of evangelism, but it is a key component. No battle strategy relies solely on one weapons system saying, 'In this regiment we use rifles; we do not believe in artillery.' It should not be a question of either/or but of both/and.

The New Testament approach seems to be a combination of 'cold-contact' (engaging complete strangers in conversation) and 'warm-contact' (sharing with people you know are already interested) evangelism. The apostle Paul, in his missionary journeys, would initially engage in cold contact evangelism. He had to. He didn't know anybody. He would preach to strangers either in the synagogue or the marketplace. But this was only the first step in his plan. His real hope was that a spontaneous sharing of the gospel would begin, spreading down the relationship networks of his listeners—exactly as happened in Pisidian Antioch in Acts 13. Paul's job was to light the fuse and then stand back and let the Holy Spirit, working down the relationship networks, do the rest. One has to light the fuse first, and that is where open-air, cold-contact evangelism comes in. It is a powerful tool God has used down through the centuries.

Fine, but what about in our century? In the next chapter we will look at how to organise and conduct an open-air meeting today.

9

How to Conduct an Open Air

Let's now look at some practical suggestions on how to run an open-air meeting: what structure it should have and how the team members should conduct themselves.

Team effort

Open-air meetings are best with a team larger than one! The advantage of having a team is, first, that it displays the body aspect of the gospel. Our message is not just 'me and Jesus' but 'me and Jesus together with you'. This is a powerful message in an alienated world soured by broken relationships. Secondly, a team is an advantage because it allows you to do much more than you could do by yourself. On your own, you can talk to a handful of individuals. A team can talk to many. On your own, you have a narrow scope of activities open to you. Basically, you can preach. Just try singing 'He is Lord' all on your lonesome on some crowded, metropolitan street corner and see how much respectful attention you merit! A team can choose from a whole host of possible presentations. Let's look at them.

Varied, fast-moving set

Plan a varied, fast-moving set lasting twenty-five minutes. The aim of an open air is not to bore people to death. We want to win their attention and keep it. Therefore the pace of the meeting should be brisk and its content varied. Twenty-five minutes is long enough to get some good content across, but not so long that people cannot stay for the duration. At the end of the set you simply disperse your team among those who have stopped to listen. Then, in twenty-five minutes you gather troops back together again, going through the same set with whatever variations you want to introduce.

Here's one suggestion as to how to organise your twenty-five minutes:

Worship/singing	8–10 minutes
Drama piece	3–4 minutes
Testimony	2 minutes
Drama	3–4 minutes
Preach	7–10 minutes

There are two types of singing: worship or proclamation. Both are good. Ask the Holy Spirit to guide the team as to which would be more relevant to your particular open air.

In worship, we forget about the crowd. The focus is on God. In this case, it is often helpful to gather in a circle. That way there will probably be less inhibitions and distractions to entering into worship. According to Psalm 22:3 (KJV), God inhabits the praises of Israel, his people. In worship we bring down the presence of God.

People can taste and see that the Lord is good. Demons flee. The spiritual atmosphere is cleared. One of our YWAM teams travelling through Greece found that the most effective way they could draw and touch large crowds was by simply worshipping God. It was more effective than drama, preaching or any other tricks they could pull out of a bag.

Singing as proclamation is also powerful and scriptural. David, in one of his frequent bursts of enthusiasm for God, exclaimed, 'I will praise you, O Lord, among the nations; I will sing of you among the peoples...let your glory be over all the earth.' Here the focus is the people rather than God himself. In worship we gather in a circle because we are addressing God. In singing proclamation we fan out in a semi-circle because we are addressing the people. We are telling through song what God has done.

You may close your eyes in worship, but don't in proclamation. You would think someone either rude or strange if they closed their eyes while talking to you. Think of yourself as talking to the crowds who stop. Look at them. Smile at them. Don't think of it as spearing them with truth; think of it as sharing good news. Pray for those who catch your eye while singing.

The dramas you do must now be slow, ponderous or 'deep'—ie not like some of the modern plays seen in the West End. They should be easy to follow, dramatic, basic in their plot, either entertaining or moving. Entertaining or moving? Definitely. Remember that it's not action and costumes that make a drama production, it's drama. And it is only drama when people's emotions have been touched. If you don't touch people's emotions with a dramatic performance, you are wasting their time. You will then find you have no audience.

Street dramas need to be overplayed. No room for

delicate nuances. You have to hit people over the head with colour, sound, action and feeling. Otherwise you may land yourself in an embarrassing situation similar to the one I once found myself in on London's crowded, noisy Portobello Road market. In the middle of a decidedly flat piece of drama, a young family came by and, seeing an open spot on the road—only open because we had cleared it for our drama—stood there and chatted to each other smack in the middle of our aspiring actors. They didn't even know there was a drama in progress! They simply assumed we were some excitable types talking slightly louder than normal as we went about our shopping. Very disconcerting to be giving it all you've got when right under your noses a foursome are avidly discussing their latest purchases, completely unaware of your heartrending efforts. They are discussing and wondering what end of the market to aim for; you know—you want to aim for the rear end!

Quiet, underplayed street dramas on a noisy and crowded street will simply get lost. They will make no impact at all.

It is also immensely helpful if the drama appears to have a meaning. That meaning needs to be clear. I once took out a team who were up in London for just a few weeks. Consequently, I had not seen any of their dramas. However, I rashly agreed to speak after their presentation. As I was watching a rather bewildering array of characters cavorting about the street in all manner of wonderful get-up, the piece suddenly stopped and I was on! I hadn't a clue as to what it was about so, starting strongly (sanctified bluff—always important for a preacher), I said, 'Ladies and gentlemen, you may be wondering what that was all about. Well, let me tell you...so am I!' And on I waffled.

Perform any deep piece, slightly esoteric in its meaning, and you will find people esoteric in their attendance.

There are numerous good books on street drama giving both scripts and general advice which you will find in your local Christian bookstore. Christian theatre groups like 'Footprints' and 'Riding Lights' and others you can ask about put out very helpful material. This is a lot easier than writing your own, at least in the early stages.

The testimony/preaching also needs to be fast-paced, clear and heart-felt. It can pick up on the point presented in the drama, but it should not belabour it. You are not meant to be making a blow by blow cultural/literary critique of the dramatic presentation, but simply using it as a launching pad for some scriptural point you feel your listeners need to hear. The testimony needs to be personal and 'the preach' needs to be challenging. We shall say more about both testimony and evangelistic preaching in Chapter Ten.

Location

There are two basic types of location for open-air work: the high street or tower block. Residential areas, aside from tower blocks, should usually be avoided as there is an insufficient concentration of people. Tower blocks can provide a setting for useful open airs, but you have to ensure that you have a good supply of colourful and action-packed dramas to pull people out from behind their curtains. You will also need a team primed and ready to go around the flats during and after the open air. Engaging people in conversation in a tower-block open air takes more work than on the high street, but it can certainly be done. Lastly, you will also need amplification, just in case you want somebody actually to hear the testimonies and preaching.

For high street open airs you want to find a spot with constantly-moving foot traffic and a spot wide enough for people to stop without obstructing foot traffic. There are few things so depressing as an open-air meeting which finds itself addressing one passer-by every two minutes. Empty spaces yawning before you which are devoid of any potential listeners, much less any actual ones, steal the oomph from your zeal. If you are trying to reach people you need to go where people are. Sounds sensible! So find a spot with a good amount of foot traffic.

In order to avoid unnecessarily annoying the shop-keepers, pedestrians and peace-keeping forces, you need to choose a spot where listeners will not obstruct traffic. The police, by law, can move you on if you are 'obstructing the highway'. 'Obstruction of the highway' is defined as 'blocking a space through which another wishes to move'. Theoretically, this means that the police can move you on if ten of you are singing in a large deserted square with not a soul listening—I know, it has happened to me—the grounds being that you are obstructing a space that someone may want to move through. Another time, in fact, I was actually arrested along with my sketchboard man. On our way to Bow Street Station I said to the zealous, rookie policeman who had nicked me, 'I know you were just doing your job, but I was just doing mine.'

The law gives a certain latitude of interpretation which the police work within. One policeman will interpret the law one way, deciding that nobody is really bothered by crowded streets, another will decide quite differently. It is their right to do so. It is also your right to talk with them and question, albeit politely, their decision. If you have been asked to move on, ask if they can suggest a better spot or ask if you can have five more minutes. You will often find them helpful at this point.

You can try applying to the local council for a permit to hold a street meeting. If you can get one all the better. Too often, though, you will find yourself sent from one office to another. Nobody wants to make the decision. In that case, forget the permission. It's not usually necessary anyway.

Scatter and engage

The open air does not finish when the set twenty-five-minute programme is over. For some it has just begun. Your team needs to be ready to scatter into the crowd and engage, not the Enemy, but whoever has been listening. Here is when God's truth can be applied very personally to each person. A person's questions can be answered, their objections met.

An open air is the easiest way in the world to approach a stranger with the gospel. The very fact they have stopped means they have some interest, even if it only stems from the novelty of what you are doing. They know what you are about when you approach them, which does away with the awkwardness of trying subtly to introduce the gospel into a conversation about some subject remote from spiritual truths, such as football or ballet. ('Talking about feet, I've got gospel shoes which you might want to hear about.') You can walk right up to someone and ask outright, 'What did you think about what we were saying?' If they say, 'Rubbish,' you can ask why. If they say they got there too late to catch your main drift, you can explain. If they say they liked it, you can go on and take it further.

Remember, people are human too

When you go up to someone in an open air, you do not suddenly transform into someone different from the person you are at the office or in your home. (I hope that's not bad news!) Christians are not meant to have 'Jackal and Hide' personalities—hiding the gospel most of the time and at official open airs coming on strong, devouring their victims. We don't become evangelistic machines.

A zealous Christian I met approached me at an open air and our conversation went something like this:

'Hi, I'm Paul.'

'Praise God, I'm saved by the blood of the Lamb.'

'Uh, yes. I'm living in London. And you, where do you live?'

'I'm resting in my Redeemer. He's my dwelling place, praise be to his name.'

'Quite, quite.'

'Brother, for God so loved the world that he gave his only Son....'

'Absolutely. Speaking about the time, I really ought to be talking to that person over there. Ciao.'

I felt like I had not met the person but, instead, had come up against a barrage of texts. God's love is not like that. It's personal. Let it flow through you. One of the nice points about approaching a person after an open air and asking, 'What did you think of that?' is that we are expressing a desire to hear their opinions, their feelings. We are not going to lay siege with a steady bombardment of Scripture...at least, not yet!

In Chapters Three and Four we looked at the importance of combining boldness and naturalness in our evangelism, so I will say no more about it here. There are, however, a few more helpful pointers which, if those

who scatter among the crowd remember, will help us to
be more effective witnesses in the open air.

Expect divine appointments

Paul writes in Ephesians 2:10, 'For we are God's work-
manship, created in Christ Jesus to do good works,
which God prepared in advance for us to do.' God has
gone before us preparing good works which we walk in
and do. That means he has prepared people for me to
meet out there during that open air. I need to keep my
eyes open, asking God to lead me by his Spirit to those
very people. Ask God for divine appointments.

How do you enter a divine appointment? One way is
by the prompting of the Spirit. You just know that you
should go over and talk to a particular individual. Once,
when I was working with Youth With A Mission in
Afghanistan, I was out buying food supplies when I
passed a bicycle rickshaw just as it was stopping. Out
stepped a young, long-haired Westerner obviously on his
way to a hotel. I had that prompting, that inner compul-
sion I could not shake off, that I should go up to him and
talk. 'But Lord,' I said, 'I don't know him and I'm on my
way somewhere else.' But the Lord does not quit that
easily. I gave in and went up to him. It turned out that he
was a non-Christian who had heard of our ministry while
in India. He was, in point of fact, actually looking for
this rumoured Christian ministry with the hopes that he
could stay there. Could I help him find it, he wondered. I
told him he had found the right man or, rather, the right
God had found him. Follow God's promptings and you
will follow him into divine appointments.

Another method of entering divine appointments is
just to follow your common sense. For instance, it does
not take much spiritual discernment to understand what

to do when, at the end of an open air, there is a crowd gathered around waiting to be talked to. Chances are that if the evangelistic team closed their eyes at the end of the meeting and prayed fervently for guidance, by the time they opened their eyes there would be no one left. Don't wait for a rainbow or tongues of fire to descend on someone's head; just wade in there and talk to the first person at hand.

We had just finished an open air at Hyde Park and most of the onlookers seemed to be engaged in conversation. I glanced about to see who I could talk to when I noticed a man dressed in black sitting near my feet. He did not strike me as promising material, looking as hard as he did. But as there was no one else to talk to, and as he seemed to be making moves to depart, I thought I had better introduce myself and see what happened.

He was more interested than he appeared. Soon we were deep in conversation. 'This is obviously one of those divine appointments,' I thought with rising excitement. After forty-five minutes of sharing I thought we had said enough and that it was time for me to go. But I kept feeling that I had forgotten something important, that though our talk was good there was something I needed to do that I was neglecting. So I stalled for a bit until all of a sudden it hit me, 'I know what it is! I haven't asked him if he wants to become a Christian yet; if he wants to repent and ask Jesus into his life!' Rather a basic oversight for an evangelist. When I asked him if he wanted to do this he said, 'Yes, of course.' We prayed right there on that spot. That day his life was turned around. Today he is a missionary in Brazil.

Direct and ready to pray

Don't make the same mistake I did. Be ready to pray with people.

Be direct with people. One advantage in meeting total strangers on the streets is that they are often ready to tell you things they would never dream of telling their nearest and dearest. They can afford to. They'll never see you again. In return, we can be more frank than we might want to be with our own nearest and dearest. We can tell them God's opinion of their lifestyle. They can take it right between the eyes if they sense you love them.

Take the example of 'Holy Hubert'—so dubbed by the radicals of the University of California, Berkeley, among whom he ministered in the sixties. He was a plug-ugly, croaky-voiced little bulldog of a preacher who pulled no punches denouncing sin in the rebellion-racked campus of Berkeley. One day, Hubert wrote:

> While I was preaching on campus, ten or fifteen of the Gay Liberation group began harassing me. I called them pitiful queers and told them that Jesus Christ could save them, and when He did they would be looking for decent women to marry.
>
> My reprimand enraged them. One young man began throwing his fist in my face, shouting, "Don't you call us queers!"
>
> "I suppose you want me to call you 'gays'," I answered, and then took off in a verbal barrage, explaining that to be gay is to be happy. "You never had a happy moment in your lives, you miserable bunch. Don't tell me that you are not queers by your own perverted wills.... Your little minds are dominated and ruled by demonic powers, making you the demonic queers you are.... Jesus Christ can cure you."[28]

How did someone like this win many to the Lord and

become admired by Christians and non-Christians alike? Because straight speaking was only one side of 'Holy Hubert'. The other side is seen in situations as described below.

> One afternoon two black militants caught me off campus and both of them jumped me. There was no one around, and they nearly killed me. Blood was streaming down my face, and I thought my jaw was broken. They kept beating me in the face until one of them said to the other, "Look, you've hit him enough. Stop it! Let him go!"
>
> "Aw, I wanna hit him just once more."
>
> My mouth was full of blood, but I remember saying just before passing out, "I love you sirs. God loves you."[29]

You can take a lot from someone who loves you like that, as is shown by what happened subsequently.

> A few days later, while walking on Bancroft Way, I met one of the men.
>
> "Good morning, my free soul," I said. It almost blew his mind. He couldn't understand how I would still be friendly after the beating he gave me. Not many days later, while I was speaking on campus, a white man started to attack me. The black man I had met on Bancroft Way knocked the white man flat on his back. He said to me, "Hubert, if anyone—black or white—ever lays a hand on you, I'll whip him like he's never been whipped before."[30]

My point is not that you should emulate 'Holy Hubert's' exact approach—he was one of God's characters who could get away with it—but that love opens a way for straight talk. Be direct with those you witness to. Tell them what God says. Call sin sin. The Holy Spirit does not put a premium on the mealy-mouthed; he anoints the truth.

And be ready to pray with people. Ask those you

have talkedd with, even if they are not ready to submit their lives to Jesus, if they would mind you praying for them. You will find that 99% will say that's fine, even if they are taken aback that you meant here and now on the street. I just assure them they don't have to pray and then I go on and say a simple prayer of blessing over them.

Not only is this valuable because God answers prayer, it is also a demonstration in itself of our personal relationship with God. We Christians have been at this so long that sometimes we can take for granted the amazing, revolutionary basics like prayer. Remember, there are some who have never prayed outside of a prayer book in their lives. They cannot conceive of prayer as simply talking with God. A simple, heart-felt prayer is a witness to our relationship to Abba, Father.

More importantly, God answers prayer. One afternoon I was witnessing to a young man who'd just moved to London and was working at the Drury Lane Theatre. It was a blustery, grey day and only a few had stopped at our open air. At the end of our talk he was still not convinced of the reality of Jesus Christ, but he did allow me to pray for him. I prayed that he would have a revelation of Christ. I then gave him my phone number. Three hours later I picked up the ringing phone to hear an excited voice yelling down the line, 'He's real. He's real!' Back at his flat, God had somehow revealed himself to him. God had answered prayer.

What about amplification?

One of the best ways in the world to get on people's nerves is to move into a confined space with your open-air team and blast them with a screechy amplifier. The

next best way is to stand across the road from the sinners—the wider the better so as to give maximum
emphasis to your belief that you are different and want
to keep apart—and bombard them with gospel texts,
preferably in the olde King James Version. You are, I
trust, catching my drift: I love amplification because of
its highly personal nature.

The rule of thumb should be: only use amplification
when you have to. If your voices are too weak, if the
space you are operating in is too large, if your crowds are
too big to address with your naked voice, then use amplification. In settings like these it suits admirably. Where it
is ridiculous is when you are bearing down with all the
megawatts modern technology can provide upon your
total audience of one blind man and his deaf dog.

Try to get a good quality system that does not distort
your voice, and only have it as loud as you absolutely
need to.

What to do if there is opposition

You cannot expect that if you go out on the streets it will
always be peaceful and quiet. Don't look for opposition,
but be prepared for it.

Hecklers are an irksome hazard, but not necessarily
deadly. As long as they are not being vile it is important
that you keep your sense of humour. If you sniff disdain-
fully at a heckler who dares to interfere with this called
and anointed preacher of God's eternal gospel; if you
come across a holier-than-thou, then you have lost it.
People will switch off. Keep your ability to laugh at
yourself.

The preacher can even trade a few friendly insults
with the heckler. Once, at London's Speaker's Corner, I
was approached by one notorious heckler who boldly

marched up to me, his doting entourage in tow, shouting, 'There you are. Who let you out? The doctors have been looking for you all afternoon. Tie him up and I'll take him back before he gets dangerous.' To which I replied, 'Michael, you rascal, you only know about it because you're from the padded cell right next to mine.'

You must not lose your temper—otherwise you will lose your testimony. People won't hear what you are saying, they will hear what you are doing. On a number of occasions I have seen dedicated preachers get fed up with a foul-mouthed heckler and decide they were ordained of God to fulfil Scripture—'so that every mouth may be silenced' (Rom 3:19)—with a well-placed thump. They enter into the same spirit as the heckler. The heckler may be lifted up, but God is not.

If the heckling is low and blasphemous then there are several things you can do. First of all, try to ignore him. You do not want to draw attention to what he is saying, you want to keep the crowd's attention on what you are saying. A heckler wants attention. If he does not get it he will go away.

Try to outshout him. Do not respond to what he is saying by dialoguing with him. That is taking him more seriously than he deserves. Keep on saying what you intended to say, but say it with more volume. Finding he cannot make a dent, the heckler may well just give up. This is especially true of inexperienced, novice hecklers.

Divert him. Have two of your team go up to him and try to draw him into conversation. This will get his attention off the bigger meeting. Be sure that you draw him away from the crowd while talking to him lest, through loud conversation, the crowd's attention be drawn away from the preacher. If the discussion gets too lively you should leave it. The point of the discussion was to divert the heckler, not to seriously discuss with him. In 99% of the cases that is a waste of time. While diversion is a good tactic, be prepared for the fact that an expert heckler will not allow himself to be drawn away like this.

Rebuke the spirit using him. Send some of your team to get near him and pray against any demonic influence. Again, on a number of occasions I have seen this used to good effect.

If all else fails, pray and ask God for help. Naturally, this is not just a last resort. It is an effective resort. One German anarchist gave us a terrible time for weeks in Leicester Square. We tried everything. He could not be diverted; he just laughed at us when we rebuked the spirits; his voice was twice as loud as mine and five times more durable. We were at our wits' end. We desperately asked God for help. One day we were having an anointed meeting with a good crowd when we spotted our German anarchist coming over. Our spirits sank. He went and stood next to a burly labourer who was clearly interested in our open air. As the German anarchist began his stream of comments, this beefy angel in disguise turned to him, stuck a threatening clenched fist under his nose and barked, 'Shaddup.' Transformation! The German's mouth snapped shut and peace reigned supreme. We never had any trouble with him after that. Walk softly and God will send somebody to carry a big stick.

Heckling is not the only type of opposition you will get. Sometimes the storekeepers or marketstall keepers will tell you that you are not only a nuisance but a distraction to their business. A stall keeper approached me once on Portobello Road, reeking of whisky, telling me to 'push off' as he was losing customers. He began to get aggressive, pushing his reddening face up against mine. To give myself breathing room, I gave him a light shove backwards. Being drunk, he stumbled and fell headlong. That's all his brother on the stall needed. Seeing the family honour was at stake he rushed out from behind his stall and grabbed my head in a headlock hold, hissing, 'That's my brother!' I responded with my by-now perfected hugging technique. He had my head, I had his chest. As well as one can when struggling energetically at close quarters, I explained that his fall was an accident due to his drunkenness.

After our little tussle had quietened down, the team prayed about what we should do. On the one hand, I did not want to concede that the gospel has no right to be preached on the street. On the other hand, I did not want to cause unnecessary aggravation. So we asked God what to do—saying we were willing to stay if that was right. On that outreach we had a large ex-Marine with us whose Christian convictions, I was now hoping, did not include pacifism! We might be needing his unique gifting and equipping! In the end, we felt God telling us to move on to another spot. When, at our new spot, somebody came to the Lord, my hope that we had done the right thing was confirmed.

But had we done the right thing in the first place? Were we being persecuted for stupidity's sake rather than righteousness' sake? Being persecuted for the gospel is one thing; it's quite another to be opposed for being a pain in the...nethermost parts. This stall keeper was not opposing us because of the gospel. It wasn't that he hated the name of Jesus and wanted to stop it being preached. He was simply losing business, or so he claimed, because of us. This thought disturbed me. I was not out on the streets to make the stall keepers lose business.

I wrestled with this question when I got home that evening. I found my answer in Acts 19:23ff. Paul caused a riot in Ephesus. The whole city rose up against him.

What stood out to me in this passage was that Paul was not being persecuted here because of the Ephesians' pure hatred of the gospel. They couldn't give a hoot for the gospel one way or the other. They did, however, care passionately about their business. It was not the gospel but the secondary, derivative effects of the gospel that aggravated the Ephesians. It was not the message of the cross, but the prospect of their idol-statue business declining which really bothered them. They would lose money! In the immortal words of Will Rogers, 'Whenever someone says, "It's not the money; it's the principle of the thing,"—it's the money!'

All this should come as no surprise. The very nature of sin is that it does not take God seriously. Sin takes itself—its own wants, desires, ambitions—seriously. God is only seriously considered when he becomes a hindrance to what we want. Only then is he actively opposed. The rest of the time he is not even bothered with.

This was even true of the Pharisees' persecution of Jesus. They did not hate Jesus because they had an inherent antipathy to the doctrines of grace. The real reason they opposed Jesus was because, 'If we let him go on like this, everyone will believe in him, and then the Romans will come and take away both our place and our nation' (Jn 11:48). Jesus was a threat to their selfish ambition, even as Paul was a threat to the Ephesians' livelihood.

So don't be surprised if you get this sort of opposition. You need to ask God for wisdom to steer between two extremes: on the one hand making an unnecessary nuisance of yourself, and on the other hand always trying to please people. Stall owners don't own the streets, the King of the universe does. He has every right to have his gospel proclaimed in his world.

What if no one stops?

Apathy, of course, is harder to bear than opposition. At least if you are getting opposition you know you are making some impression. So, what should you do if no one stops and it seems you are making little impression?

First, you should persevere a bit longer. Things may come right, given a bit more time. I have been in open airs where initially not a soul stopped and, by the end of the meeting, found a good crowd had gathered.

Secondly, you might stop the meeting in mid-motion and gather the troops to pray. Send them around the square or street praying in twos. Gather together again at a designated time to share what God has been saying and to recommence the open air.

Thirdly, consider doing something completely different. Maybe you need to break out of a rut. Consider scrapping the open air altogether and sending your team members around in twos to witness to people one to one (two to one) as they meet them. Maybe you should do a praise march up and down the street instead.

Clear the cobwebs! Think creatively! We are all prone to doing the same thing in the same way at the same place so often that we dig a rut for ourselves. The means replaces the end. Open-air meetings are only one means among many to reach people with God's love and God's truth.

Joe Ellis relates this story demonstrating how activities lose their original purpose—'We've always done it this way!'—get set in concrete and become a meaningless tradition.

When Bismarck of Germany was making an official call on the Czar of Russia, he noticed a guard standing, for no apparent reason, in the middle of the lawn. Bismarck inquired about the reason for the sentry. The Czar admitted he did not know why, but for as long as he could remember, guards had stood at that spot twenty-four hours a day. The Czar questioned other members of the staff about the tradition. No one knew the reason for it. The captain of the guard, finally, was able to discover the reason.

Several decades before, the Czar's grandmother had noticed a wild flower blooming at that spot on the lawn and ordered a guard posted to keep careless feet from trampling it. The little flower was long since gone, but no one rescinded the order; no one questioned the tradition. Two generations later, sentries were still being posted at the spot, twenty-four hours a day, seven days a week, fifty-two weeks a year—for no reason whatever.[31]

Let's not allow open-air work to become just another tradition. It deserves better than that.

Open-air work can be fun and exciting. Open-air work can make a real impact for God. If we are going to have effective open airs we are going to need effective preaching and meaningful testimonies. Chapters Ten and Eleven go on to look at how to prepare testimonies and evangelistic sermons.

IO

Preaching

'People of Amsterdam,' John's voice rang out above the milling crowds, 'God loves you.' John Goodfellow, YWAM evangelist based in Amsterdam, is one of the most effective street preachers I know. Yet consider this entry I found the other day in my diary.

> August 17, 1976
> The outreach has been going well. Last Saturday droves of people stopped, especially to hear John; which just shows how slow one must be to form an opinion about someone's abilities. Before this week he [John] had been bad and I was wondering and doubting that he should even be street preaching.

Preaching is a human skill to be developed as well as a divine gift to receive. Don't think that because the first time you got up in the open air it was a complete disaster, there is no hope for you. We have to develop our gifts. Human skill cannot replace a divine gift, but practice and experience can enhance it.

There have been some players elected European Footballer of the Year who are what are called 'natural footballers'. Holland's Johann Cruyff was like that. He was a natural footballer who instinctively knew the right moves. Other winners were more like Liverpool's Kevin Keegan. He was not so much a purely instinctive player as he was a hard-working player. Through diligent practice he developed the more ordinary natural talents he had until he, too, became the best in Europe.

Preaching is much the same. You can develop yourself. You will never develop yourself beyond your gift, but you can maximise your gift.

Threefold task

Your task as you face an open-air crowd is threefold: to win people's attention; to give them understanding; to challenge them to a decision. If you do not win their attention none of the good things you have to say will benefit them. They won't be listening. So get their attention.

You also want to give them understanding—understanding of who God is, what he has done for man and what he expects of man. Faithful witnessing means more than quoting Scripture. They probably won't understand what the Scriptures mean. Certainly this was true of the Ethiopian eunuch who was asked by Philip, ' "Do you understand what you are reading?" . . . "How can I," he said, "unless someone explains it to me?" ' (Acts 8:30–31). We have to take the Scriptures and make them available, relevant and important to our hearers.

Communication is not what you say, it's what they hear. If what we are saying—in quoting Scripture—is heard by the crowd as irrelevant nonsense, then we are not communicating.

John Stott speaks of preaching as bridge-building. He writes,

> It is because preaching is not exposition but communication, not just the exegesis of a text but the conveying of a God-given message to living people who need to hear it, that I am going to develop a different metaphor to illustrate the essential nature of preaching...that of bridge-building...a bridge is a means of communication between two places which would otherwise be cut off from one another.[32]

Lastly, we need to challenge for a decision. 'Choose for yourselves this day whom you will serve,' thundered out God's prophet in days gone past (Josh 24:15). God's message today is no different. We are not speaking to entertain people or to provide interesting theories for speculation. We are serving people with God's summons. There is a decision that needs to be made. The world needs to be made aware of that.

Helpful guidelines

But if that is where we are going, then how do we get there? What goes into constructing an evangelistic message? Let me give you seven 'rules' that should help you on your way. These rules are not inflexible, but should be regarded in the same light as most motorists seem to regard traffic regulations, ie as 'helpful guidelines'.

Rule 1: have something to say

Preaching has been described as: 'The art of saying nothing at great length.' You may be able to get away with this indoors, with a captive audience, but it will never do in the open air.

'Aim at nothing and you will hit it.'

Focus what you have to say upon two or three main points. Don't diffuse your energies among fifteen different points. Better to say two things well than to say ten things badly.

If you have ever been dragged through a museum you are not interested in, you will know what it is like to endure a message with multiple points, each one of them insufficiently developed. After an hour of trudging down museum hallways, glancing left, right, left, right at picture after picture—as if in training for a Wimbledon centre court seat—your heart slows, your eyes droop, your feet drag, your hands hang listlessly at your side, your mouth opens in a permanent yawn. Friend, you're beat! This is the effect of diffusing attention among too many points.

How different when you have one or two clear points that you hit with all your might. The shotgun approach, scattering points everywhere, says a lot but penetrates little. The rifle approach, firing one shot precisely, goes deep and hits just where you want it.

The additional advantage of having a message with a clearly defined focus is that you are more likely to remember what it is you wanted to say! This is no small advantage when you are facing a crowd who want to hear your next point and expect you to know what it is!

You really cannot take sermon notes into the open air. It is just not suitable for the casual, rough-and-ready environment. It will separate you from your listeners, making communication even more difficult.

Not only must you have a clear focus, knowing exactly what you want to say, it must also be worth saying. In your preparations, as you are mulling over different points, ask of them that awkward little question, 'So what?' Challenge each of your points to show you why they should be presented. If they satisfactorily pass the 'So what' test then they are probably worth telling.

Charles Spurgeon, in lecturing his students on preaching, gave this sage advice about open-air work.

To dwell long on a point will never do. Reasoning must be brief, clear, and soon done with. The discourse must not be laboured or involved, neither must the second head depend upon the first, for the audience is a changing one. Each point must be complete in itself. The chain of thought must be taken to pieces, and each link melted down and turned into bullets: you will need not so much Saladin's sabre to cut through a muslin handkerchief as Coeur de Lion's battleaxe to break a bar of iron. Come to the point at once, and come there with all your might....

In the streets a man must from beginning to end be intense, and for that very reason he must be condensed and concentrated in his thought and utterance. It would never do to begin by saying, "My text, dear friends, is a passage from the inspired word, containing doctrines of the utmost importance, and bringing before us in the clearest manner the most valuable practical instruction. I invite your careful attention and the exercise of your most candid judgment while we consider it under various aspects and place it in different lights, in order that we may be able to perceive its position in the analogy of faith. In its exegesis we shall find an arena for the cultured intellect, and the refined sensibilities. As the purling brook meanders among the meads and fertilizes the pastures, so a stream of sacred truth flows through the remarkable words which now lie before us. It will be well for us to divert the crystal current to the reservoir of our meditation, that we may quaff the cup of wisdom with the lips of satisfaction.".... If you go out to the obelisk in Blackfriars Road, and talk in that fashion, you will be saluted with, "Go on, old buffer," or, "Ain't he fine? MY EYE!" A very vulgar youth will cry, "What a mouth for a tater!" and another will shout in a tone of mock solemnity, "AMEN!"

If you give them chaff they will cheerfully return it into your own bosom. Good measure, pressed down and running over will they mete out to you. Shams and shows will have no mercy from a street gathering. But have something to say, look them in the face, say what you mean, put it plainly, boldly, earnestly, courteously, and they will hear you.[33]

Digest and apply that advice and you cannot go far wrong.

Rule 2: illustrate

The great nineteenth-century revivalist Charles Finney said, 'The truth not illustrated is as likely to convert sinners as a mathematical demonstration.'

In saying this he was only following in the footsteps of another famous preacher about whom it was said, 'He did not say anything to them without using a parable' (Mk 4:34). Jesus always used illustrations (parables) when he taught. This was no accident of style. Jesus made a conscious effort to illustrate his otherwise abstract points. Love, faith, etc were just words unless he could bring them down onto terra firma with illustrations from everyday life. You can hear the wheels turning, can see his mind working overtime to come up with an apt illustration in Luke 13:18: 'What is the kingdom of God like? What shall I compare it to?' We need to make the same kind of effort.

The saying goes that one picture is worth a thousand words. It's absolutely true. Spurgeon helpfully points out that illustrations are like the windows of a house and: 'The chief reason for the construction of windows in a house is...to let in light. Parables, similes, and metaphors have that effect; and hence we use them to illustrate our subject, or, in other words, to "brighten it with light," for that is Dr. Johnson's literal rendering of the word "illustrate".'[34] The *Oxford English Dictionary* defines 'lustre' as 'the quality of shining by reflected light'. So when we 'il-lustre' a point we are making it shine by shedding light on it.

Illustrations not only shed light, they give interest. Everybody loves a good story. Illustrations prevent your message from being dry. Of course, it has to be an apt illustration. If the illustration is corny then I am afraid your point will be made corny.

Illustrations are all around us if we will only have eyes to see. Get them from your own experience, from biographies you read, from the newspaper. When you talk about the emptiness of sin, mention that recent celebrity's suicide everybody is talking about. When you talk about the peace only God can give, mention the Christian aeroplane pilot shown on the front page of the newspaper with a terrorist's pistol at his head, and tell his testimony of perfect peace in that horrific situation. These are situations the general public know about and so will be interested in.

Illustrations, touching stories, also have the power to move hearers in a way that unillustrated doctrine is unable to. General Booth was a veteran of the street and his comments on the importance of moving our hearers was this: 'I use various means to create a certain impression upon the hearts, to be frankly emotional up to a point. I desire to produce that heart opening without which I believe it to be of little use making an appeal either to the intellect or the conscience.'[35]

DL Moody, another nineteenth-century evangelist much used in both Britain and America, used to preach 'layer-cake' sermons. He alternated layers of illustrations with layers of points. He would give a long and touching story and then bring out of it the spiritual truth he wanted to impress upon his hearers. He would repeat this maybe three times and that would be his sermon. Often Jesus preached in this layer-cake fashion. In some of his sermons the bulk of his talk was taken up by the illustration.

Use them.

Rule 3: use your imagination

The imagination is a powerful tool. Those of you who have seen *Jaws* will remember that the scariest bits were not those where you actually saw the oversized brute, but when you didn't see him! It was when the sea was quiet and unruffled with only the first hints of that ominous 'da-dum, da-dum' swiftly picking up its crescendo that your own nerves thrilled and your heart beat wildly. You started, involuntarily gripping your companion's arm, and, then recovering, whispered, 'Don't be silly. It's only a film.' Your eyes didn't see the shark, but your imagination was supplying the details.

Use this power of imagination in communicating the gospel. A friend of mine sometimes starts his open-air sermon by standing on a cardboard box and shouting at the top of his voice, 'Oh no, I don't think it's going to hold me. Can anybody help me?' People are curious, wondering what in the world is going on. Gradually, the box crumbles and, to the crowd that has now gathered, he explains that this is what it is like to build our lives or anything else than God our Rock.

People imagine that they know what the boring old gospel is about. We, who know they do not, sometimes have to use shock tactics to get them to see it differently. Use your imagination as to how you can surprise them, catch their attention and present the gospel from a fresh angle.

Make your illustrations live with the power of your imagination. Don't tell your stories, relive them. Imagine yourself as one of the characters in your story. How did they feel? What was going on around them?

These are the details that make the story real. Don't say 'the situation was tragic'. That's too abstract. Describe the tragic details that make the listener say, 'Oh, that's tragic.' CS Lewis wrote a letter in 1956 to a child in America in which he gave this advice:

> Don't use adjectives which merely tell us how you want us to feel about the thing you are describing. I mean, instead of telling us a thing was "terrible", describe it so that we'll be terrified. Don't say it was "delightful", make us say "delightful" when we've read the description. You see, all those words (horrifying, wonderful, hideous, exquisite) are only saying to your readers "please will you do my job for me". [36]

George Whitefield knew how to make his illustrations take wing. He knew how to supply the vivid detail necessary to kindle the imaginations of his listeners. If he did not know the quote, he certainly knew the truth of the Arabian proverb which runs, 'He is the eloquent man, who turns his hearers' ears into eyes.' Lord Chesterfield, the sceptical rake infamous for his published letters to his son schooling him in the arts of seduction, used to love to hear Whitefield preach. On one occasion Chesterfield was in attendance at Whitefield's Chapel where, his biographer tells us, the following scene unfolded:

> Whitefield was describing the sinner by likening him to an aged and blind beggar. The old man is being led by a little dog on a cord and feels his way by tapping the ground before him with a cane. Directly before him, however, there lies a great yawning chasm, but as he approaches it he loses the dog's leash and as he reaches the edge of the precipice

the cane drops from his hand. He lurches forward to retrieve it but his foot falls only on empty air—but at that point, Chesterfield, overcome in visualizing the old man's plight, leapt to his feet crying, "He's gone! He's gone!"[37]

Chesterfield was gripped because Whitefield dramatised his story, illustrating it with vivid detail. Go and do thou likewise.

Rule 4: illustrate, explain, apply

Employ the general structure: illustrate-explain-apply. Catch people's attention with an illustration. Explain the point of the illustration. Then apply this point to their lives. The point is not that your message should come out in a neat three-step progression. The point is that you know what elements to include in your message and what to look for in constructing a message.

I will outline one of my open-air messages to show you how I might go about illustrating/explaining/applying. On the left-hand side are the notes as I would actually write them on a bit of paper stuck in my pocket. On the right-hand side, in parentheses, are comments I would not have on my bit of paper but which I include here in order to clarify the meaning of my headings.

—Tourist or Merchant	(Ask the crowd which one they are in life. An interest teaser. Act out a tourist gawking. Ask if profit from life or just look.)
—Everything Costs	(Ask if they have learned this basic lesson. Act out silly scene of buying something and then amazed when actually expected to pay for it.)
—Pyrrhic victory	(Refer to King Pyrrhus who gained a victory but at too

great a cost. Ended up actually losing the war though won battle. Apply: 'You doing that?' Have everything but unhappy—illustrate with own testimony or something in the news.

Then quote Matthew 16:26 re 'gain world, lose soul'.

—You more 'n body   (If you grow fat, not more of you essentially...if chop arm off, not less of 'you'. Illustrate with actions. You're a soul.)

—Made for God   (Ultimate cost is separation from him. Talk about what Jesus did to solve separation...bit of personal testimony. Challenge listeners to respond.)

This entire little message is woven around one theme of 'cost'. It's simple, concrete and understandable to someone who has never been to church. I also sprinkle it liberally with illustrations.

Keeping a stock of quaint quotes is also extremely useful. If I am talking about the emptiness of sin I might use a quote by AE Matthews, 'In the end I got so old and tired and weary of living, that I looked in *The Times* obituary column each morning—and if I wasn't there, I got up.' If I am talking about atheism, I might use Bishop Fulton J Sheen's statement: 'An atheist is a man with no invisible means of support.'

Sprinkle in a dose of humour if you can. I have already mentioned 'Holy Hubert', who was not only a straight-talker but a pungent wit.

One day a young man pushed towards him screaming,

'Hubert, it takes an idiot to be a Christian! It takes an idiot to be a Christian!'

'You qualify! You qualify!' was the quick response.

On another occasion Hubert was explaining how out of the heart are the issues of life. Someone fired back, 'Hubert, you know the heart just pumps blood...Life is in the brain.'

'Young man,' Hubert replied, 'I heard of a man who supposedly had his brain removed and still lived.'

'How can a man live without a brain?'

'You don't seem to have any problem,' Hubert shot back.[38]

How do you choose a topic for your message? Take anything that strikes you. It may be a scripture, an observation from nature, a newspaper clipping. Ask how your point is significant to your non-Christian listeners. Ask: 'So what?' Sit down and illustrate it, explain it and apply it. You then have a message. Pray over it and give it with all you've got.

Rule 5: preparation is vital

Mark Twain once said, 'It takes me three weeks to prepare a good impromptu speech.'

Paul Miller says, 'You cannot present a jewel you have not first dug out.'

When you stand up in the open air you should not stand up with an empty head. Don't think that God is more likely to anoint you and fill you with his thoughts if you empty yourself of all your own thoughts. Ralph Lewis tells the story of the minister

who wanted to be so sensitive to God's leading that he made a habit of only preparing the first half of every sermon. That way, he reasoned, he'd allow God to show him where to go and what to say during the second half.

One day he was sharing this strategy with one of the

laymen in his congregation. The man listened to the preacher, thought for a moment, and then said, "I guess I ought to congratulate you then, pastor. Your half of the sermon is invariably better than God's."[39]

You will not necessarily use everything you have prepared. That's unimportant. Your preparation will set you off in the right direction. You can veer from it, should you want to. It may be that in the middle of sounding off on your prepared points you will have a sudden, new inspiration. Give it, by all means.

I have found that 80% of the spontaneous inspirations that have come to me on the spur of the moment are actually the fruit of past meditation and preparation. Only about 20% are totally new, never-though-of-before points. The Holy Spirit has simply reminded me of something already stocked in my memory. The Holy Spirit is the householder who brings 'forth out of his treasures things new and old'. You first have to store treasure away so that the Holy Spirit can then bring it out. Prepare your messages.

Preparation means work. It means keeping a lookout for good illustrations. It means reading. It means keeping a file of newspaper cut-outs. It means keeping a file index so that you have a record of what you have saved so far. (What is the good of saving things you cannot find when you need them?) This work and preparation will reward you with messages that communicate.

One other point: '*Steal, steal, steal!*' Just because a thought is not yours does not mean you cannot use it if it's good. Truth is not invented, it is discovered. It does not belong to the person who discovered it any more than it belongs to you.

Samuel Johnson once said, 'Your manuscript is both good and original; but the part that is good is not original, and the part that is original is not good.'

Be more concerned with being good than original. Use the vast storehouse of insights, quotes and illustrations that others can give us. See what others have used to communicate effectively and then copy it. That is how we will learn, by emulating our betters. 'Imitate me,' the apostle Paul says. Good advice. Follow it.

Rule 6: manner is almost everything

It was Charles Finney who said, 'Manner is almost everything.' How you say it is almost as important as what you say. Think of your own conversational manner and you will see this is true.

What if you proposed to your girlfriend in a wooden monotone voice, eyes staring glassily into space as you repeated robotically, 'I...am...fond...of...you.... Will...you...marry...me...my...dear?... I...await ...your...response...'? She is not likely to be too impressed. Or what if you tried to convince someone how worried/uptight/twisted up inside you were—as you lounged languidly on the sofa, nonchalantly whistling a tune? Our manner needs to suit our subject.

Some psychologists say that the emotional impact of any message is:

55% facial and body
38% vocal intonation
7% verbal, what you say[40]

Great preachers not only communicated by their content, but by their manner. When George Whitefield was asked by a friend if he could print his sermons, Whitefield replied, '...if you like, but you will never be able to put on the printed page the lightning and the thunder.'[41]

The best way to have a presentation that is appropriate to your message is to be totally taken with your message. Then you will naturally strike the right note, and your style will enhance what you are saying rather than detract from it.

Here are a few other observations.

Look at people. Don't look at the sky, the building or, worst of all, the ground. You are a preacher addressing people, not a St Francis addressing the birds. When you talk to people, look at them.

Do not mumble. Lift up your voice and try to speak clearly. In the early days I was most frustrated because my wife would tell me she could not hear me while standing only ten feet away. I learned, with time, how to project my voice more effectively. You will too as you build up experience.

Do whatever arm strokes or dramatic gestures come naturally to you. People are very different here. I am an Anglo-Saxon by background, but with a maverick Italian streak somewhere: I have to be gesticulating with my hands or I just know I am not communicating. Ask your friends who have watched you for a time if you have any particularly annoying gestures that you would be better off without.

Preach it! Declare the word of God. God does not give us the 'Ten Suggestions' nor does he, in inviting us to the marriage supper of the Lamb, say, 'I know you are busy and I hate to take you away from other more pressing business, but I wonder if you could possibly spare a moment to pop in for just a tick. Awfully good of you if you could make it.' No, he issues an unequivocal, 'Come!' You are not out there to air your questions, but to tell God's answers. You are not standing up to give your considered opinions, but God's final and revealed word. During your illustrations is the time to be light and low-key, but when you come to making your main points, make them! As we said earlier, have something to say and say it.

Besides these few points, you needn't give much attention to style. An artificially cultivated style is no key to effective communication. Let yourself be taken with your message and most things will come right.

Rule 7: preach Jesus

It does not matter how you get there, but preach Jesus. You may not start by talking about Jesus, but you want to end up speaking about him. It is Jesus who saves; he who must be believed in; he who is the centre of the gospel.

The gospel is really very simple: 'Believe in the Lord Jesus Christ and you will be saved.' A person does not have to understand all about the different theories of the atonement or how many judgements and resurrections there are. He has to repent of his sins and believe in Christ.

The great evangelist, DL Moody, had only recently been converted when he applied for church membership. Tongue-tied during his examination by the elders, the best he could do in answering their question, 'What has Christ done for us all—for you—which entitles him to our love?' was a feeble, 'I don't know. I think Christ has done a great deal for us. But I don't think of anything particular as I know of.'[42] He was refused membership.

The thief on the cross did not have the time to develop a systematic theology on the person and work of Christ. It is doubtful whether he would have passed a test on the meaning of atonement. He just believed in Jesus. He saw Jesus as the hope and light of his world. His unconventional 'sinner's prayer' went like this: 'Jesus, remember me when you come into your kingdom' (Lk 23:42). That was good enough for Jesus—'I tell you the truth, today you will be with me in paradise.'

Focus on Jesus. 'You who bring good tidings to

Jerusalem, lift up your voice with a shout, lift it up, do not be afraid; say to the towns of Judah, "Here is your God!" ' (Is 40:9).

Be of good cheer

Don't be discouraged if you have not seen any evidence of conviction and conversion by the end of your open-air meeting. God could well be working where you do not see.

Albert was a member of our ministry team in London who, one weekend, went off to a conference with his denomination. Albert got talking with his conference roommate and discovered that he lived in the Nottingham area. After Albert explained what our team in London did—open airs, etc—his roommate said, 'You're not, by any chance, working with some people called Paul and Jamie [my other key street preacher, now in London but originally from Nottingham], are you?'

When Albert said that was exactly who he was presently working with, his roommate excitedly said, 'Well, you tell them this story. I went into Nottingham to do my shopping and, as I crossed the square, I heard someone shouting. I stood at the fringe of the crowd and listened, intrigued, to the entire gospel message. No one came up to talk to me, but I left determined to know more about this gospel. For over a year I read every book I could get my hands on. Now I am a Christian. I learned later, after they had left Nottingham, that the team leaders of that open air were Paul and Jamie. Tell them, "Thank you, and keep up the good work." '

God is working even when we are not working. Ask him to work during the open air and believe him to do just that.

II

The Gospel According to Me

We were all gathered in Leicester Square listening to a young girl give her testimony of coming to faith in Christ. From her nerves it was obvious that she had never done this before in such a public setting. At that moment a band of three hecklers approached our group. I feared for this young, innocent looking girl as I knew how merciless these hecklers had been to some of our other preachers.

The hecklers just stood watching for a while so I sidled over to them, hoping to be of some use...not to them but to the girl. After a while, instead of launching into a diatribe against the girl, they just looked at each other and said, 'Aw, she is so vulnerable. I can't do 'owt.'

The honesty and simplicity of a testimony is powerful. It moves people. It cuts through scepticism and cynicism. The listener may not believe, but it is evident that the one giving the testimony does. A sincere testimony waylays the accusation of 'hypocrite' so often thrown at those with a belief in Christ.

An experienced preacher can appear professional, smooth, confident—maybe, therefore, preaching for ego reasons or because it is his job. It is obvious that these motives do not apply to a sincere, heartfelt testimony.

A testimony carries authority because of its evident sincerity. A testimony also carries the authority of personal experience. We are not now sharing what someone has told us, we are sharing our personal experience with Christ. The saying goes, 'The man with an experience is never at the mercy of the man with an argument.'

One reason Jesus had an authority that the Pharisees did not have was because he had experienced the truths he expounded. 'I tell you the truth, we speak of what we know, and we testify to what we have seen' (Jn 3:11). Jesus had seen what he was speaking about.

As stated earlier, giving a testimony, witnessing to our faith is simply a matter of telling what we have seen and heard. 'You will be his witness to all men of what you have seen and heard' (Acts 22:15). It involves telling what Christ means to you; why he is meaningful to you personally; how he has made a difference in your life.

Sharing your testimony is not the same thing as preaching. You ought not to get up and expound John 3:16 (except incidentally as it fits into your own personal story), digging out the Greek roots and commentators' alternative translations. You are not so much expounding the gospel according to John as you are the 'gospel according to me'.

A personal testimony is simply a restatement of the Acts sermons (see Acts 2:31–32; 4:10; 5:30). Their basic message was, 'He's alive!' A personal testimony shows this exact point. It shows Jesus alive in the twentieth century changing lives.

I once was rebuked by a well-meaning Christian for talking about myself. (Here I am, still at it!) He said I should not talk about myself, but only talk about Christ—'For we do not preach ourselves, but Jesus Christ as Lord' (2 Cor 4:5). But God also said, 'Return home and tell how much God has done for you' (Lk 8:39). He was instructed to talk about God's dealings in his own life. Tell God's actions now, not just in the days of Noah and Moses. He is as much the God of today as he is the God of the past and the God of for ever. People need to know that.

In 2 Corinthians 4:5, Paul is saying that our ultimate aim must be to glorify God, not ourselves. He is saying that ultimately our message is all about what God has done, not what great Christian ministries have done. He is not saying that it is a sin to ever utter that word 'I'. No, glorify God by telling what he has done for you.

The beauty of testimonies is their variety. There are as many different testimonies as there are Christians. We need this wide variety of testimonies to relate to the wide variety of non-Christians that are listening. Your testimony will speak to somebody in a way that no one else's can.

Do not denigrate your testimony because it is not one of those 'I-was-a-junkie-at-age-three-gang-leader-at-eight-and-a-bad-bad-dude-flush-with-girls-Cadillacs-and-cocaine-freak-outs-by-the-time-I-was-eleven.' A non-Christian hearing that sort of testimony could well say, 'Boy, he needed to get saved! I'm sure glad I'm not like that.' He might not be able to relate to that testimony, but he may well relate to your more 'ordinary' testimony. Thank God for how he has dealt with you. Don't be ashamed of it. Don't make up juicier add-ons to spice it up. Tell it like it is.

Prepare, cook and deliver

Work on giving a two- to three-minute testimony that you could give in the open air. Do not leave this any more to spontaneity than you would your open-air sermon. It is more difficult to pack two or three minutes with meaningful material than it is a ten-minute slot. You have no time to waffle. You have to strike gold right away. So preparation is important.

Divide your testimony up into three parts: before, during and after. Tell what your life was like before Christ. There will be some listening who will be able to identify with you on this point. They will be thinking, 'That's like me!' This also raises interest. Human interest stories always fascinate people.

Then tell how Christ became real in your life. Tell what happened. Let them know that Christ is a living Person who changes people today.

Lastly, tell them how your life is different today because of this encounter. Is this experience still current in your life or is it solely something out of the murky past? Has Jesus made a concrete, practical difference? Yes? Then explain how.

You only have three minutes so you cannot give a developed autobiography which beings, 'Well, it all started before I was even born with my great-grandmother Lizzy....' You have to select highlights, specific events which illustrate what you are talking about. Pick out one mood or problem you struggled with before your conversion. Tell an incident that happened to you, showing in real life what that problem was doing to you. Then pass on. That's about all you have time for. It's time to tell what Jesus did now. Tell of something concrete. Give a specific illustration from your life. You can only pick up threads, but if you pick up the right threads you will communicate powerfully.

Lastly, emphasise relevant material. If I am giving my testimony to a largely Catholic audience, I do not major on, 'I used to be a Catholic, but now I am a Christian.' That would just put barriers up. I share that part of my experience which I think is most relevant to my listeners.

Paul did just this in Acts 22 when he shared his testimony with the Jewish crowds. He said, 'A man named Ananias came to see me. He was a devout observer of the law and highly respected by all the Jews living there' (Acts 22:12). What was Paul doing here? He was highlighting something in his testimony that would make it easier for his listeners to receive what he was saying. If he had been speaking to a Gentile audience he would probably have dropped all mention of Ananias' good Jewish credentials because there would have been no point.

Let your testimony be a blessing to other people. Tell what God has done for you.

Yikes, what now?

Have you ever been in that awful situation where you have been witnessing and sharing your testimony with somebody for a good while, and when you ask them whether they would like to become a Christian, they say, 'Yes'? Yikes, what do you do now? You don't want to blow it. You want to lead them to Jesus, not to never-never land and beyond. How do you lead someone to Christ? If you have a pre-set plan which takes a person who wants to become a Christian through the vital steps, you will be much better prepared for this moment.

I like to use a little four-step plan that the late Rev David Watson used to use. It is clear, comprehensive and easy to remember.

1. Something to admit

Romans 3:23—'For all have sinned and fall short of the glory of God.' Mankind not only has a problem with God; God has a problem with mankind. We have failed him, rebelled against him and gone our own way. Step one is to admit this.

2. Something to believe

1 Peter 2:24—'He himself bore our sins in his body on the tree . . . by his wounds you have been healed.' Watson suggests illustrating this by placing a book in our hand demonstrating a blockage between our hand and the sky. Then the right hand (=Jesus) takes away that book/blockage as in Isaiah 53:6. Where are the sins now? Gone!

3. Something to consider

Luke 14:27–28—'And anyone who does not carry his cross and follow me cannot be my disciple . . . first sit down and estimate the cost.' Jesus must be Lord as well as Saviour. We cannot separate these two functions. We take God as he is—God and Lord—or we do not take him at all.

4. Something to decide

Revelation 22:17—'The Spirit and the bride say, "Come!" . . . let him take the free gift.' There is something for us to do. We do not simply wait for God to save and forgive us. When we lift our hearts to God in repentance and faith he responds. This is where you can lead a person in prayer.

Some people are quite happy to pray out spontaneously. Many, however, have never prayed out loud, at least not with someone else present, and will need help. This is where it is often helpful to have them follow you in prayer as you lead phrase by phrase. As long as they mean the words it does not matter that the words originally come from you. God still hears them!

Use this little outline and see if it does not help you when somebody says, 'Yes, I would like to become a Christian. How do I do it?'

12

Apologetics in Evangelism

In 1974, four English youths passed through Amsterdam on their way to Iran where they expected to be initiated into the alluring and mystic art of astrology. They never made it! Instead, they went for dinner at a Christian outreach ministry there—two houseboats called 'The Ark'.

Over dinner they began discussing astrology with Mike Saia, the resident brain and Bible teacher. Absorbed, heads locked in conversation, they disappeared after dinner to continue their discussion in some quiet corner.

Upon reappearing several hours later, I was informed by their ringleader that as a result of their very helpful discussion they no longer believed in astrology!

'So you now see where astrology is wrong, and you understand why it is false?' I asked.

'Not really,' came the reply. 'We didn't understand a word Mike was saying, but *he* certainly seemed to know what he was talking about!'

That's apologetics!

Hopefully, however, it is more than that. Apologetics is more than discombobulating the opposition with high-flying nonsense (or even with low-flying nonsense!). Apologetics is giving the unbeliever reasons for our faith. It is doing what the apostle commanded in 1 Peter 3:15—'Always be prepared to give an answer [*apologia*] to everyone who asks you to give the reason for the hope that you have.'

We Christians not only have a hope, we have a reason for our hope. A hope without a reason is no more than an exercise in wish fulfilment. The apostle Peter was exhorting Christians to show unbelievers that their faith was much more than wish fulfilment; to show that their faith was based on realities versus dreams.

Christianity is based on a grand fact; a confrontation with a set of facts that could not be wished away. In 1 John 1:1 it says, 'That which was from the beginning...which we have seen with our eyes, which we have looked at and our hands have touched—this we proclaim concerning the Word of life.' The basis of our faith is not some high-minded and elusive first principles, but a very concrete man that could be seen and touched.

There is a reason for our faith. Jesus saw to it that there was. In Acts 1:3 we read, 'After his suffering, he showed himself to these men and gave many convincing proofs that he was alive.' Faith is not opposed to reasons and 'proofs'. In fact, the apostles' faith was founded on reasons and proofs.

Jesus said, 'Believe me when I say that I am in the Father and the Father is in me; or at least believe on the evidence of the miracles themselves' (Jn 14:11). Jesus offered evidence. His method was not to say, 'Just believe,' trusting that if he said it often enough and loudly enough people would follow. No, he said,

'Believe,' and then proceeded to give them some reasons why they should.

The apostle Paul was also more than a 'just believe' man. We see him in Thessalonica's synagogue where he 'reasoned with them from the Scriptures, explaining and proving that the Christ had to suffer and rise from the dead' (Acts 17:1–2). He was reasoning and proving as well as proclaiming. He was responding to their particular questions and difficulties so that they too would have a reason to believe.

Paul knew that people do not believe something without a reason. They need a faith founded on fact. They need fundamental objections and questions answered. This is the task of apologetics.

Apologetics is not 'apologising for our faith'—an activity for which no lessons are necessary—but is rather 'defending our faith'. *Apologia*—the root word for 'apologetics'—is a Greek word meaning 'verbal defence'. Sometimes it is translated 'answer'. (See its use in Acts 25:16; 1 Corinthians 9:3; 2 Timothy 4:16.) Paul not only preached the faith, he defended it. He said, 'Here's what I believe, why I believe it and why you should believe it too.'

Granted, you cannot prove your way into faith. After all the reasons have been presented, miracles seen and objections answered there is still a step of faith that needs to be taken. We still have to step out and say, 'I believe.'

But if you cannot prove your way into faith you can clear the ground for it. Apologetics does just this. Faith comes from considering Jesus. Apologetics clears the way for considering Jesus by addressing those intellectual doubts (the 'pie in the sky' syndrome) which hinder people from taking Jesus seriously.

We should neither claim too much nor too little for

apologetics. It is not *the* key to evangelism but neither is it unimportant. It is a key that will fit some doors and not others. Some people need to have their questions answered, while others need to have them exposed for the smokescreen that they are. Sincere questions need answering; evasive smokescreens need blowing away.

Proverbs 26:4–5 gives us some simple advice: 'Do not answer a fool according to his folly, or you will be like him yourself. Answer a fool according to his folly, or he will be wise in his own eyes.'

So what is it to be: answer him or not answer him? The first half of this little riddle is simply saying that we should not be drawn into foolish discussions; in foolishly discussing we are acting like fools. Avoid unfruitful conversations. Do not take people's objections more seriously than they deserve. With some people, their real problem is their attitude, not their objections.

Notice how the apostle Paul, in addressing objections to God's hardening of hearts in the Old Testament, focused on the attitude behind the objection rather than on the objection itself. He said, 'But who are you, O man, to talk back to God?' (Rom 9:20). He saw that the real issue was their lack of a fear of God rather than their lack of understanding. To be drawn into discussing the objection would have been foolishness.

In the second half of this proverb, the writer was saying that there are times when, rather than avoiding foolish objections, the objector ought to be answered; the aim being to put him firmly in his place, show him his folly. This is what Jesus did to the 'clevers' in Luke 20. Three times they tried to catch him out and three times he answered in such a way that 'no one dared to ask him any more questions' (Lk 20:40). He was making them look too bad! Finally, Jesus launched an initiative himself, stymying them with his question about how the

170

person referred to in Psalm 110;1 could be both David's son and Lord (Lk 20:44). That drove the final nail in the coffin. Jesus had Proverbs 26:5 down to a fine art.

The teachers and priests in Luke 20 were determined not to believe. Their questions were not genuine, but were designed to embarrass Jesus. The contrast could not be greater than with the Bereans who 'were of more noble character...and examined the Scriptures every day to see if what Paul said was true' (Acts 17:11). Note that they did not immediately believe. But nevertheless they were commended because they enquired with a sincere heart 'if what Paul said was true'. It is with this sort of person that apologetics can be successfully pursued.

Objections

There are four main objections to the Christian faith which I have encountered on the streets and we will spend the rest of this chapter looking at them. They are:

1. All religions are the same.
2. Jesus was just a good man.
3. You cannot trust the Bible.
4. If God is a God of love, why does he allow suffering?

1. All religions are the same

'What's the big to do about converting to Jesus? All religions are basically the same.' If I have heard it once I have heard it a thousand times.

Take the usual formula—'Religions have superficial differences (how many times they pray, their particular form of prayer, what foods they are allowed to eat, etc), but they are basically the same'—stand it on its head, reverse it 100% and you have something much closer to the truth. I say that religions are superficially identical, but radically different at their roots.

It is true that most religions push a belief in a higher power, duties of honesty, mercy to the poor and a spirit of devotion. But giving to the poor and being nice is not what makes a man a Hindu or a Muslim or a Christian. This is not the central core of his religion. It is the fruit and not the root of his faith. It is the superstructure and not the foundation.

At the heart of any religion are the basic questions.
—Who is God?
—Who is man?
—What is the basic problem in the world?
—What is the answer to this problem?

A religion is defined by the answers it gives to these questions. If we take three different belief systems— Christianity, Hinduism and Western naturalism (the operative belief system of our modern, secular world)— and compare their answers to these basic questions we shall see that they are radically different.

Who is God? Christians say he is a personal God (has intellect, emotions and will) who is separate from his creation.

Hindus say he is an impersonal God, a 'force' not at all separate from his creation. His creation is him, just in a lower form. (This is called Pantheism.)

Naturalism differs slightly in that it thinks this question unimportant and unanswerable!

Who is man? Christians say man is an eternal creature of infinite worth who has been made in the image of God. He is like God but he is not God.

Hindus (of the more philosophical schools that have been exported to the West) say that man is actually God, indeed, that everything is God.

Naturalists say that man, far from being made for

eternity in the image of God, is no more than a glorified animal evolved from the apes. 'When you're dead, you're dead,' is the naturalist's startling new insight.

God, man or animal—which is it to be? One thing is for sure: the answers are very different.

What is the basic problem in the world? Christians say the basic problem is sin. Man, though he knows better, has rebelled against God and consequently lost his way.

Hindus say that the basic problem is ignorance, 'maya'. The problem is not that man has rebelled against God, but that he has forgotten he is God! He is suffering from cosmic amnesia, the absent-minded professor taken to absurd lengths.

Naturalists are no longer sure what the problem with the world is! They used to think it was lack of education, lack of civilisation, lack of technology, lack of money or lack of expert potty training in infancy. Nobody knows any more.

What is the solution to the problem? Christians say the solution is the cross of Christ which needs to be embraced in repentance and faith.

Hindus have several solutions—meditation, a devotional life, chanting. The common thread tying together all their solutions is that they emphasise man's good works. They are not focused on what God has done for man, but on what man must do for God. They are not focused on a once-for-all act of God to forgive man— Jesus' death on the cross—they focus on the process man must go through to get himself right with God.

Naturalists, not knowing what the basic problem is, haven't a clue as to what the solution is. There are as many solutions as there are naturalists. One thing is for sure, the one realm they will deny as a source of a real solution is the supernatural.

No differences in religions? The opposition could not

be more stark between the Humanist Manifesto which states, 'No deity will save us, we must save ourselves,'[43] and the psalmist who said, 'I do not trust in my bow, my sword does not bring me victory; but you [God] give us victory' (Ps 44:6–7).

In each of the four basic areas very different answers are given. To insist therefore that all religions are the same is a display of deliberate obtuseness of the I've-already-made-up-my-mind-so-don't-confuse-me-with-the-facts variety. True, all religions are similar in that they talk about God, ultimate meaning, good and evil. But *what* they say about them is radically different.

To say: 'All religions are the same,' is like saying, 'All political parties are the same.' Tell that to Maggie Thatcher or Tony Benn! True, both Labour and Conservative parties have similarities—both believe in a democratic, parliamentary procedure; both aspire to prime ministerial office—but what they want to do once in power is quite different.

Some say, 'All religions are the same,' from an ignorance of the deeper issues addressed by religions; some because their underlying conviction is actually that what one believes is unimportant. What counts is the integrity with which you pursue your belief. The Religion of Sincerity! 'To thine own self be true,' etc. But here is the problem: while the motive behind this new religion is a charitable effort to transcend the 'petty' differences of warring worldviews, the actual result is just one more warring worldview on an already overcrowded field. Far from bringing harmony, far from saying, 'You are all right. You are all saying the same thing in different ways,' this Religion of Sincerity ends up saying, 'You are all wrong! What you have died for and lived for all these centuries is actually unimportant.'

'All religions are the same' is a lovely cliché but an

awful lie. It needs to be dismissed for the superficially clubby, Auld Lang Syne arms-around-the-shoulders-and-forget-our-differences myopia that it is.

2. Jesus was just a good man

We were at Hyde Park's 'Speaker's Corner' where one of our girls was on her soapbox telling the crowd how Jesus could not have been just a good man. He was either Lord, liar or lunatic. Larry, a Canadian on his way through London on his summer tour of Europe, thought she made eminently good sense. He stopped to consider the claims of Jesus more seriously. Very dangerous! Within a few days he was a Christian. Today he is doing mission work in the Pacific Islands.

All too many believe that Jesus was a great man 'like Buddha or Mohammed', a sort of religious genius. Relatively few agree that Jesus was absolutely unique. This can only be because relatively few have honestly considered his claims.

CS Lewis wrote:

> "I'm ready to accept Jesus as a great moral teacher, but I don't accept His claim to be God." That is the one thing we must not say. A man who was merely a man and said the sort of things Jesus said would not be a great moral teacher. He would either be a lunatic—on the level with the man who says he is a poached egg—or else he would be the Devil of Hell. You must make your choice. Either this man was, and is, the Son of God: or else a madman or something worse. You can shut him up for a fool, you can spit at Him and kill Him as a demon; or you can fall at His feet and call Him Lord and God. But let us not come with any patronising nonsense about His being a great human teacher. He has not left that open to us. He did not intend to.[44]

Once one looks at Jesus' astounding claims it becomes

175

clear why Lewis said what he did. Consider John 6:38–40: 'For I have come down from heaven...to do the will of him who sent me. For my Father's will is that everyone who looks to the Son and believes in him shall have eternal life, and I will raise him up at the last day.' Come down from heaven? The author of eternal life? Raising people up? Is Jesus suffering from delusions of grandeur? These claims, perfectly understandable if Jesus is divine, are the height of presumption if Jesus was just a good man. Good men are humble!

Jesus' listeners reacted with the same 'Who does he think he is?' that twentieth-century crowds would have responded with. John 6:42 records their exact words: 'Is this not Jesus, the son of Joseph...? How can he now say, "I came down from heaven"?' They were offended by his presumption. But what is highly presumptuous for man is perfectly ordinary for God.

Lunatic or Lord, which is Jesus? Was Jesus suffering from a megalomania on the scale of Field Marshal Montgomery's who, when asked the identity of the three greatest commanders in history, replied, 'The other two were Alexander the Great and Napoleon!'?

Jesus would not leave well enough alone. He kept up his steady barrage of outrageous claims.

In John 10:19 the Jews had had enough, finally dismissing Jesus as raving mad! Given the choice was between lunatic or Lord, they opted for lunatic. They knew that Jesus' claims were too out-of-this-world to be absorbed with: 'He's a great moral teacher.' You either rejected them out of hand or knelt down to worship him.

In Matthew 10:34–35 Jesus said, 'I did not come to bring peace, but a sword. For I have come to turn "a man against his father, a daughter against her mother...."' Again Jesus provoked the question, 'Who does he think he is? What right does he have to spoil the

most precious human relationship there is: the family?'
Only God has that right. Exactly.

Jesus went on to say in verses 37–39, 'Anyone who loves his father or mother more than me is not worthy of me . . . whoever loses his life for my sake will find it.' Isn't this a bit rich if Jesus was just a man? He claims he deserves more love than our own family! He said we should willingly—even cheerfully—give up our lives and spoil our earthly prospects for him. More, he put himself on a level above us when he said that otherwise we are not 'worthy' of him. Worthy of him! Who does he think he is? Precisely! He is either liar, Lord or lunatic.

The above is only a smattering of the astounding claims Jesus made. He claimed to forgive sins, to deserve worship, to exist from eternity, to be the key to the salvation of the human race; on and on Jesus went, with complete aplomb, calling attention to his powers and his importance. What would have been arrogant presumption in man was simple humility in God. For a three-year-old to claim, 'I can drive,' is foolhardy presumption; in an adult it is commonplace. Whether we see pride or humility depends on our perception of the identity of the claimant. So it is with Jesus. What is not on is to ignore his claims and then to say these claims—whatever they are—are perfectly ordinary. They aren't.

3. You cannot trust the Bible

The complaint runs like this: 'Have you ever played the game where you gather in a circle and whisper something into the ear of the person on your left, with instructions to send the same message on to the next person, who whispers it to the next person and so on till it goes right around the circle? By the time it comes back to you your original story is invariably changed. That's what the

Bible is like. It's thousands of years old. We cannot trust its accuracy.' True or false?

First, let's respond by remembering the issue here is not the inspiration of the Scriptures. That's another battleground. The battle here is about historical accuracy and reliability. Is the gospel we believe today the same as was believed in the first century? Can we be confident that there ever was a historical figure called Jesus of Nazareth?

In *Evidence that Demands a Verdict* Josh McDowell cites the four basic principles of historiography: the bibliographical test, the internal evidence test, the external evidence test and confirmation by archeology. The reliability of secular documents is tested in this way. How does the Bible stand up to these tests?

(a) The bibliographical test. How good is the textual transmission? How many reliable copies exist? What is the time interval between the original document and our earliest surviving copy?

See the following table and you will get a good idea of just how reliable the Bible really is.

Author	When Written	Earliest Copy	Time Span	No of copies
Caesar (Gallic Wars)	100– 44 BC	AD 900	1,000 yrs	10
Plato (Republic)	427–347 BC	AD 900	1,200 yrs	20
Thucydides (History)	460–400 BC	AD 900	1,300 yrs	8
Aristotle	450–385 BC	AD 900	1,200 yrs	10
God (New Testament)	40–100 AD	AD 350	200 yrs	2

The *Codex Sinaiticus* (AD 350) contains the complete New Testament and 50% of the Old Testament. It is found in the British Museum in London.

The *Codex Vaticanus* is dated from AD 325–350 and contains all the Bible in Greek. It is housed in the Vatican.

The *Codex Alexandrinus*, also in the British Museum, contains the entire Bible and was written in the fifth century.

The *Codex Bezae*, in Cambridge University Library, was written in the fifth or sixth century. It contains the gospels and Acts in both Greek and Latin.

There are in existence about 5,000 Greek manuscripts of the New Testament in whole or in part. We have a wealth of material, much of it of very early origins. This means that the reliability of the biblical manuscripts is actually much better than all the other classical texts. Nobody doubts Caesar's account of the Gallic Wars and whether these events ever took place. So no one should doubt, on bibliographical grounds, whether the biblical events ever took place.

(b) The internal evidence test. The document is presumed innocent unless proven guilty. It is assumed to be telling the truth unless there are obvious contradictions and known factual inaccuracies.

The Bible is not full of contradictions and impossibilities. To the ever-popular question, 'Who did Cain marry?' the simple, unpopular answer is, 'One of his sisters' (see Genesis 5:4).

What about the very different genealogies for Jesus given in Matthew 1:1–17 and Luke 3:23ff? John Haley responds,

> Mary, since she had no brothers, was an heiress; therefore her husband, according to Jewish law, was reckoned among

her father's family, as his son. So that Joseph was the actual son of Jacob, and the legal son of Heli (Mary's father). In a word, Matthew sets forth Jesus right to the theocratic crown (throne of David); Luke his natural pedigree. The latter employs Joseph's name, instead of Mary's, in accordance with the Israelite law that "genealogies must be reckoned by fathers, not mothers."[45]

The much ballyhooed contradictions of the Bible can all be ironed out with a bit of careful examination and study. There are many good books such as J Haley's *Alleged Discrepancies of the Bible* which address this problem for the serious enquirer. The Bible passes the second bibliographical test. It is internally consistent.

(c) the external evidence test. Do other historical materials confirm or deny the documents' internal testimony? We have stunning verification of the events of the New Testament out of the mouth of the enemies of Christianity.

Lucian, a satirist of the second century AD, wrote (in *Death of Peregrinus*, 13) the following:

> ...the man who was crucified in Palestine because he introduced this new cult into the world...Furthermore, their first lawgiver persuaded them that they were all brothers one of another after they have transgressed once for all by denying the Greek gods and by worshipping that crucified sophist himself and living under his laws.[46]

This contemporary of the early church vehemently disagreed with Christian doctrine, but he never questioned the actuality of Christian events.

And Cornelius Tacitus, historian and governor for Rome of Asia, wrote in his Annals (15.44) around the year AD 112:

Therefore to scotch the rumour [that Nero had started the fire], Nero substituted as culprits, and punished with the utmost refinements of cruelty, the class of men, loathed for their vices, whom the crowd styled Christians. Christus, from whom they got their name, had been executed by sentence of the procurator Pontius Pilate when Tiberius was emperor; and the pernicious superstition was checked for a short time, only to break out afresh, not only in Judea, the home of the plague, but in Rome itself, where all the horrible and shameful things in the world collect and find a home.[47]

Tacitus seems to have regarded Rome as a kind of first-century California! Of greater interest to us is his view of the Christians. He was evidently no fan of theirs. Of even greater interest to us is that he never dreamed of denying that Christians, Christ, Pontius Pilate, or the crucifixion were historical realities. He did not doubt it; why should we? Surely these second-century historians were better placed than we, eighteen centuries later, to determine what happened in Palestine.

At one time it was thought that the historical unreliability of the Bible was demonstrated through its frequent mention of the nation of the Hittites (see Genesis 23:10; 26:34; Joshua 11:1-9, etc). No other documents mentioned them. The Bible was obviously wrong! Then, in 1906-7, 10,000 clay tablets were found documenting the life of a powerful nation called the Hittites who in 1800 and 1400-1200BC rivalled the Mesopotamian and Egyptian kingdoms.[48]

The Bible was not behind the times, it was ahead of the times.

(d) Confirmation by archeology. There is a multitude of archeological confirmation of biblical events, but we will have to content ourselves with one exemplary story

taken from the reminiscences of Major Vivian Gilbert, a British army officer:

> In the First World War a brigade major in Allenby's army in Palestine was on one occasion searching his Bible with the light of a candle, looking for a certain valley. His brigade had received orders to take a village that stood on a rocky prominence on the other side of a deep valley. It was called Michmash and the name seemed somehow familiar. Eventually he found it in 1 Samuel 13 and read there: "And Saul, and Jonathan his son, and the people that were present with them, abode in Gibeah of Benjamin but the Philistines encamped in Michmash." It then went on to tell how Jonathan and his armour-bearer crossed over during the night "to the Philistines' garrison" on the other side, and how they passed two sharp rocks: "there was a sharp rock on the one side, and a sharp rock on the other side: and the name of the one was Bozez and the name of the other Seneh" (1 Sam 14:4). They clambered up the cliff and overpowered the garrison, "within as it were an half acre of land, which a yoke of oxen might plough". The main body of the enemy awakened by the melee thought they were surrounded by Saul's troops and "melted away and they went on beating down one another" (1 Sam 14:14–16).
>
> Thereupon Saul attacked with his whole force and beat the enemy. "So the Lord saved Israel that day."
>
> The brigade major reflected that there must still be this narrow passage through the rocks, between the two spurs, and at the end of it the "half acre of land". He woke the commander and they read the passage through together once more. Patrols were sent out. They found the pass, which was thinly held by the Turks, and which led past two jagged rocks—obviously Bozez and Seneh. Up on top, beside Michmash, they could see by the light of the moon a small flat field. The brigadier altered his plan of attack. Instead of deploying the whole brigade he sent one company through the pass under cover of darkness. The few Turks whom they met were overpowered without a sound,

the cliffs were scaled, and shortly before daybreak the company had taken up a position on "the half acre of land".

The Turks woke up and took to their heels in disorder since they thought that they were being surrounded by Allenby's army. They were all killed or taken prisoner.

And so, after thousands of years British troops successfully copied the tactics of Saul and Jonathan.[49]

The Bible is so factually accurate that it can even serve as a vital topographical guide to military strategists millennia later.

4. If God is a God of love, why does he allow suffering?

For multitudes facing the death of loved ones or reading the news bulletins, the 'problem of pain' is more than a delicious brain-teaser; it's a deeply-felt gut issue. One South London grandmother, having just witnessed the death of her eighteen-month-old grandson, spat out at me, 'Don't ever tell me there's a God.'

Is God just to allow such suffering? More, is God loving to allow such suffering? Millions the world over shout, 'No!' How can we answer them?

Of course, knowing how to answer is secondary to knowing how to minister. The last thing a grieving person needs to hear is a glib apologetic from some well-meaning Christian intent on setting the record straight. Comfort, affection, identification with the pain, a listening ear and a helping hand—all these come first.

Consider what helps a wailing child who comes running to you after having bashed his knee through some silly, ill-thought-out manoeuvre. Lecturing the child on his irresponsibility ('You shouldn't have been in the courtyard in the first place!') or explaining the mechanics of why he is hurting ('What do you expect if you go crashing into walls? You are going to get hurt when you run into things') helps not one iota. But throw your arms around him, give him a cuddle while murmuring, 'Ooh, I know it hurts. I know,' and that Niagara of tears magically dries up while off skips the merry child to his next activity. Comfort soothes the pain; only then are people ready to listen to exhortation and explanation.

CS Lewis, in his book *The Problem of Pain*, wrote: 'When pain is to be borne, a little courage helps more than much knowledge, a little human sympathy more than much courage, and the least tincture of the love of God more than all.'[50]

God met the problem of pain head-on, not by sending an apologetic, but by sending his Son. And of his Son it is written, 'Jesus wept.' He wept upon seeing Lazarus cold, stiff and lifeless in a tomb. In weeping for Lazarus he was weeping for a whole world where death reigned; where all that was precious bore the whiff of mortality; where the dreams of a lifetime could be cut off in a moment; where friendships were snuffed out in their prime and lovers separated by an unbridgeable chasm; where the departed beloved's throaty laugh was but a fading memory, the expired child's warm and trusting grip simply an ever-receding, hazy recollection never more to be felt in this world. Death laughed its hollow laugh over the fragile hopes of mankind. Jesus wept seeing all this. Paul said, 'Meanwhile we groan' (2 Cor 5:2). God feels for man. Our response to those in pain is no reflection of the character of God should it not convey this compassionate heart of God.

Having said that, there still remains the intellectual problem of pain. Is God just to allow suffering? Secondly, is God loving to allow suffering? In the limited space allotted me I can do no more than sketch out the briefest outline of an answer. First, let's examine the injustice issue.

God is only unjust in allowing suffering and death if

we have (1) a right to life and painlessness, (2) a right to relationship with others and (3) a right to be free from the consequences of others' actions. An injustice is a denial of what is our due. Are we due any of these three 'rights'? No, they are all gifts of God which he can give and take away as he pleases. That is his right. He is God.

Man gets into trouble when he usurps God's place and puts himself in the centre of the universe. Taking centre place in the universe is problematical—we are not universal enough! Sitting at the centre where he was never meant to be, man's vantage point gets twisted, his perspective goes haywire. This is what happened to the above mentioned grandmother. Her hurt and grief were altogether proper. Her bitterness about God was not. It arose because she would not allow God to be God (the essence of sin). Her 'rights' meant more to her than God.

Abraham, in contrast, let God be God and was willing to yield back to God the son God had given him in the first place. His son belonged to God. God had every right to claim back what was his. Nothing unjust in that.

Job's complaint was no different from this grandmother's: 'Why do the innocent suffer?' As the book of Job unfolds we see that the answer to this complaint is not found in a denial of any such innocence, in insisting that one must be suffering for one's own sins. God rebuked Job's friends for taking this line (Job 42:7). The answer lies in an entirely different direction. The answer lies in letting God be God.

God answers Job, not with some long philosophical disquisition (what this chapter is slowly turning into!), but simply by revealing himself in all his God-ness, saying, 'Where were you when I laid the earth's foundation?' and so on (Job 38:4ff). After line upon line of such irony-laced questions Job finally bows saying, 'My ears had heard of you but now my eyes have seen you. Therefore I despise myself and repent in dust and ashes' (Job 42:5–6). Job saw that God was God and that he had every right to dole out plenty or leanness.

We have said that we have no right to life or to painlessness. It is also true that we have no right to live as independent islands. There is nothing unjust in the fact that we live in a world where it is possible to suffer the consequences of others' sins—either directly, as when we are punched by somebody, or indirectly, as when a baby is killed in a volcanic mudslide. The Bible, of course, relates these outbreaks of a hostile world to the fact of the Fall; to one man's sin whose consequences are being visited on all of us.

We take the rough with the smooth. Nobody complains when they benefit from the contributions of the rest of the human race—inventions, food production, friendship, culture, books, the gift of life itself—when positive consequences come their way. Can one really fairly complain about this system of consequences when they turn out to be negative?

The fact that one man's actions can influence another for good or evil is a reflection of the significance of man and of the social nature of man. Man's choice is significant. It makes a real difference. As a social animal it makes a real difference to the lives of others. The only way to get rid of the possibility of negative consequences is to get rid of man's significance or man's social character. Either one would be too high a price to pay.

A world where love is possible is, of necessity, a world where pain is possible. Someone once said, 'If you don't want to get hurt, never under any circumstances love anybody.' Thankfully, God did not build his universe on this principle. He would rather have love with the possibility of pain than painlessness without love.

Our own poets say something to the effect that it is 'better to have loved and lost than never to have loved at all'.

God saw nothing immoral in bringing the consequences of one man's action upon another. Indeed, because of one man's sin God cursed the entire earth so that succeeding generations would have to fight this earth for their very survival (Gen 3:17–19). In addition, all would die because of this one man's sin. Was this just to Adam's descendants? It would only be unjust if we had a right to be free from the consequences of others' actions. But we have no such right. If we did we never would have been born. What is birth but the consequence of someone else's action?

In fact, a world in which each man was an island, untouched by the actions of others, untouched by what they thought, felt or did, would be a far more horrific world than the one in which we now live. Another name for such a world is hell.

Let's move on. If God is just to allow suffering and death, is he loving? After all, love goes beyond simple rights and duties; it does not simply skip by, doing what is strictly necessary. If God is acting completely within his rights to stand by and watch epidemics and wars, is he loving in doing so?

I think there are three basic responses to this: we have trivialised the word 'love'; God allows pain as a poor second option; God is not 'standing by' but has indeed done something momentous.

To think of love only as kindness is to trivialise it. CS Lewis wrote:

What would really satisfy us would be a God who said of anything we happened to like doing, "What does it matter so long as they are contented?" We want, in fact, not so much a Father in Heaven as a grandfather in heaven—a senile benevolence who, as they say, "liked to see young people enjoying themselves" and whose plan for the universe was simply that it might be truly said at the end of each day, "a good time was had by all"....

I might, indeed, have learned, even from the poets, that Love is something more stern and splendid than mere kindness: that even the love between the sexes is, as in Dante, "a love of terrible aspect".[51]

Bringing pain is no sure guide to a lack of love. The dentist brings pain, not because he hates us, but because he wants to help us. Parents inflict the pain of spanking—otherwise known as 'applying the rod of instruction to the seat of learning'—not because they hate their children, but because they want the best for their children. People go through exhausting aerobics and other forms of twentieth-century masochism not because they hate their bodies, but because they love them and want to improve them.

We willingly accept pain when the trade-off is a greater good at the other end. God does the same.

Another important consideration in looking at how a God of love can allow suffering is that this world of woe is not God's first choice. Eden was his choice, east of Eden was man's (Gen 4:16). God set before Adam and Eve a clear choice. What they took was up to them.

God allows suffering and death, but he does not like it any more than we do. Jesus' response to the death of his friend Lazarus was direct and unequivocal: 'Jesus wept' (Jn 11:35). He did not stoically look on, musing, 'Oh well, we've all got to go sometime.' No, his whole being rebelled at this imposition upon God's spoiled universe.

We should never try to 'explain away' suffering and death in the sense of making out there is no real problem to get upset about. God gets upset about it. 'Jesus wept.' There is a problem. But God is not to blame.

Jesus wept, but he also let Lazarus die. Upon hearing of Lazarus' fatal illness he had deliberately stayed put for two more days, thus leaving Lazarus to expire (Jn 11:5–6). Here's where our world doubts God. They dismiss his weeping and see only his two-day delay. They say, with the cynics in John 11:37, 'Could not he who opened the eyes of the blind man have kept this man from dying?' (It is unlikely that anyone left unconvinced of Jesus' power and compassion after witnessing a blind man's sight being restored will be much impressed even by the raising of dead Lazarus.) How easily Martha and Mary could have accused him of a lack of love. But they didn't because God's will was more important to them than their own desires; because they knew that allowing pain was not fundamentally a denial of love; and because they trusted Jesus.

Jesus wept yet he allowed Lazarus to die. He thought it was for the greater good to allow death its sway (see John 11:4). And, do you know what? The vast majority of the human race agree exactly with God's assessment. Despite our moans of, 'How can God allow such suffering?', we think, on balance, this world a good place. If we thought this world so horrible we would quit this life and commit suicide. Some do just that, but only a tiny fraction. The vast majority think living is better than dying; that, on balance, this world offers more good than woe. The fact that most of us desperately cling to life is a compliment and unintended display of gratefulness to God. Unwittingly, the human race is saying that God has been good and loving in the way he has set up his creation. Do actions speak louder than words? Well then, by our act of clinging to life we show that despite all the evil we believe God has made a good world. We like his world and we like being here. Even the unbeliever, then, answers the 'problem of pain' in God's favour.

Lastly, let us remember that God is not 'standing by' indifferently. Never! He has done something about the pain and suffering of the human race. He loves us so much he was willing to pay the greatest price possible. He sent his very own Son to suffer and die in man's place. Death couldn't beat Jesus, Jesus beat death. And this victory was all for man's sake. God was already eternal. He did not need to beat death. But man *was* under the sentence of death. And for him Jesus came. Having sent his Son, the Father was still not finished. He then sent his Holy Spirit into the world to help bring something of heaven onto earth here and now. He heals, he comforts, he guides. God has never simply stood by and watched man go to hell.

Here we have a problem. Many do not believe that God has sent his Son into the world and that his Son can make a real difference. Thus it appears to them that God has done nothing. The non-Christian asks, 'Why doesn't a God of love do something to help?' The Christian answers, 'He has. He sent his own Son.' The non-Christian replies, 'I don't believe it.' Discussion over! You cannot go any further. The solution to his problem is the very thing he won't let you give. This is as frustrating as the following:

'Mum, if you loved me you would do something about my headache.'

'Son, I went out and bought you some Paracetemol. Take one.'

'Pills! I hate pills! Besides, what can that little thing do for my head? Forget 'em. Oh, please, please help me with my headache!'

'But son, these *will* help. They are just what you need.'

'No way. You don't love me any more, do you?' (Son sulks out of room while mother shakes her head in exasperation.)

If someone says, 'I cannot believe in a God who sits by and does nothing while this world goes to hell,' then I say, 'I can't either. But that's not the God of the Bible.' God has done something so unbelievable that many people don't believe it! But that's their failure, not his.

Not only has God done something in the past—sent his Son—and not only is he doing something by his Spirit in the present, God will solve the problem of pain once and for all in the future. The Bible says God will destroy death at his coming (1 Cor 15:26) and: 'He will wipe every tear from their eyes. There will be no more death or mourning or crying or pain, for the old order of things has passed away' (Rev 21:4).

Our view of the future determines how fair and tolerable we judge our present life. Present suffering and pain only turn to despair when we lose hope for the future. Victor Frankl, Austrian psychiatrist and survivor of the Nazi death camps wrote:

The prisoner who had lost faith in the future—his future—was doomed. With his loss of belief in the future, he also lost his spiritual hold; he let himself decline and became subject to mental and physical decay....

"Give-up-itis" [would occur]...[prisoners] refused to get up and go to work and instead stayed in the hut, on the straw wet with urine and faeces. Nothing—neither warnings nor threats—could induce them to change their minds. And then something typical occurred: they took out a cigarette from deep down in a pocket where they had hidden it and started smoking. At that moment we knew that for the next forty-eight hours or so we would watch them dying. Meaning orientation had subsided, and consequently the seeking of immediate pleasure had taken over.[52]

But God has a wonderful future for the human race, if only we would embrace it. Suffering needn't throw us into despair. Suffering, anguish, separation, injustice and death do not have the last word. God does! Life and happiness do. That is why the apostle Paul could exuberantly write, 'Therefore we do not lose heart.... For our light and momentary troubles are achieving for us an eternal glory that far outweighs them all' (2 Cor 4:16–17). Put on one scale all our momentary injustices and pains (no use denying they are there) and then put on the other scale God's eternal blessings and the winner was obvious. Paul saw eternity and so he never lost heart.

It was in seeing eternity that the psalmist, grappling with the question of why the wicked prospered, got his answer. He wrote:

But as for me, my feet had almost slipped; I had nearly lost my foothold. For I envied the arrogant when I saw the prosperity of the wicked. They have no struggles; their bodies are healthy and strong. They are free from the burdens common to man; They are not plagued by human ills. Therefore pride is their necklace.... When I tried to understand all this, it was oppressive to me till I entered the sanctuary of God; then I understood their final destiny (Ps 73:2–6, 16–17).

The psalmist saw that ultimately crime does not pay because, in eternity, God collects his bills. In New Testament terms: 'We must all appear before the judgment seat of Christ, that each one may receive what is due to him for the things done while in the body, whether good or bad' (2 Cor 5:10). Justice will be done. Nobody gets away with anything.

The apostle Paul never lost heart, nor did he ever succumb to bitterness in the face of much suffering. His secret was that he knew a God who had done something about it in the past, was working on it in the present, and would be doing something final in the future. That's the God of the Bible. That's the God people need to know about.

In 1974 I met some missionaries from Iran who told me the following story. One day their three children—aged ten, twelve and thirteen—went out swimming with friends. On the way they had a horrific car crash and all three were instantly killed. The parents were devastated. The silent house and empty bedrooms daily proclaimed their loss. One evening they were going through the twelve-year-old girl's artifacts. They came across her Bible, of which she had been an ardent reader. Leafing through it they turned to the last page where, at the end of the Book of Revelation, the publishers had printed 'The End'. But what these two parents found was this: their little twelve-year-old, in a flash of insight, had crossed out 'The End' and in its place had written 'THE BEGINNING'. The beginning!

God will wipe away every tear and make all things new. He sets a hope before us. He will not settle for a world where man is dominated by sin and death. He loves us too much for that. He sent Jesus to start a revolutionary overthrow of the sin and the death gripping our planet; a revolution to be consummated at his Second Coming on a date as yet undisclosed. Now that's good news.

One more thing

We've had the problem of pain, now we need to tackle the problem of relatives (not of the mother-in-law variety, but of the 'no absolutes' variety). So pervasive is this thought form that we shall devote the whole of the next chapter to it.

13

Absolutely No Absolutes

'How could you be so presumptuous to say you know the truth? Isn't it unmitigated arrogance to say you are right and other religions are wrong?' So wrote one of my relatives upon hearing my new-found conviction that Jesus was 'the Way, the Truth and the Life'.

Jesus—with his black and white statements of: 'No-one comes to the Father except through me' (Jn 14:6) and: 'For wide is the gate and broad is the road that leads to destruction, and many enter through it. But small is the gate and narrow the road that leads to life, and only a few find it' (Mt 7:13–14) cuts right across the relativism of our day.

Make no mistake about it: relativism—the conviction that all truth is relative and that there are no absolutes—is the spirit of the age.

Paul Johnson, in his book *Modern Times*, writes:

The modern world began on 29 May 1919 when photographs of a solar eclipse, taken on the island of Principe off West

Africa and at Sobral in Brazil, confirmed the truth of a new theory of the universe. It had been apparent for half a century that the Newtonian cosmology, based upon the straight lines of Euclidean geometry and Galileo's notion of absolute time, was in need of serious modification....

Einstein himself summed it up thus: "The Principle of Relativity".... At the beginning of the 1920s the belief began to circulate, for the first time at a popular level, that there were no longer any absolutes: of time and space, of good and evil, of knowledge, above all of value. Mistakenly, but perhaps inevitably, relativity became confused with relativism.[53]

Allan Bloom adds his own personal observations as to the pervasiveness of relativism. Bloom, for years a professor of social thought at the University of Chicago, writes, in his best-selling book, *The Closing of the American Mind*:

There is one thing a professor can be absolutely certain of: almost every student entering the university believes, or says he believes, that truth is relative. If this belief is put to the test, one can count on the students' reaction: they will be uncomprehending. That anyone should regard the proposition as not self-evident astonishes them, as though he were calling into question $2+2=4$.... That it is a moral issue for students is revealed by the character of their response when challenged—a combination of disbelief and indignation: "Are you an absolutist?"...uttered in the same tone as "Are you a monarchist?" or "Do you really believe in witches?"[54]

Relativism is the new orthodoxy. Where one used to be burned for being heretical one now gets cold-shouldered for being orthodox. Orthodox Christian faith is not so much considered wrong as simply outside the right-or-wrong department. You are no longer allowed

196

even to ask whether a faith is true or false. Whether it is 'true for you' is all that matters.

It is because of relativism that such lip service is paid to the twentieth-century virtue of 'tolerance'. To be 'intolerant' or 'narrow minded' is almost as bad as being branded with that dreaded epithet 'middle class'.

Civility is highly prized by the uncertain; so someone said somewhere. GK Chesterton remarked, 'The curious disappearance of satire from our literature is an instance of the fierce things fading for want of any principles to be fierce about.'[55]

I was once at a garden party, telling a painter from New York that I was a Christian missionary. His response? 'Wonderful!' he said, with genuine feeling. But his sympathetic response in no way meant that he thought what I was doing was wonderful in that Christianity was the truth and therefore ought to be spread abroad. He simply meant that it was good that I was being true to myself and that, at least, I wasn't doing something stodgily boring like painting...houses!

This is not Christian tolerance. Christian tolerance and charity are rooted in strong convictions. Pagan tolerance is rooted in scepticism about all convictions.

Tolerance actually becomes dangerous if it does not operate within the framework of truth. There are some things we need to be intolerant about. Truth tells us what these things are.

Tolerance isolated from truth not only becomes dangerous, it turns silly. The poet Robert Frost described the ever-tolerant liberal 'as the man too broadminded to take his own side in an argument'. And what could better exemplify the modern spirit of easy-going tolerance than Marilyn Monroe's statement: 'I just believe in everything—a little bit.' Relativism may begin with scepticism, but it ends in gullibility. Without firm standards for truth, the ridiculous cannot be separated from the sublime.

The tolerance of the modern relativist is only skin deep. How annoying that Christians are pilloried as narrow-minded bigots while your blushing relativist, exuding bonhommie to all and every creed, modestly steps onto the pedestal as our new cultural hero. But don't cross him!

Bertrand Russell once said in a radio interview: 'My position is agnostic.... I'm not contending that there is not a God. What I'm contending is that we don't know that there is.' Not dogmatic? What nonsense. If I was to reply that I knew there was a God he would dogmatically reply, 'You can't.' He simply shifts his dogmatism to a different level. He is dogmatic about what people can and cannot know. Russell thought Christians were silly to hold the faith they did and he said so. He had definite views on the matter. Nothing wrong with that, but it is a far cry from being undogmatic. Russell's view seems to have been that he was not sure whether God existed and therefore nobody else was allowed to be sure either.

Dogmatic scepticism is called 'having your cake and eating it too'. While holding firmly to one set of beliefs you still appear open-minded and tolerant. How convenient! No wonder it is so popular.

The agnostic playwright, John Mortimer, once interviewed the Catholic writer, Graham Greene. At one point Greene said to Mortimer, 'I suppose you could describe me as a Catholic agnostic...on the whole I think there's a sporting chance that God exists.' Mortimer's response to the interview is enlightening. He says, 'I thought of all the conversations I had ever had about religion, and Graham Greene, taking his sporting chance on God, came nearest to a faith I could understand. I left not entirely sure of the difference between a devout atheist and a Catholic agnostic....'[56] Mortimer feels most at home in this sort of faith because it is riddled with scepticism. It is so tolerant as to be a non-faith. He likes it, though in the end he confesses he finds it difficult to discern the difference between this faith and his doubt. That's because there is no difference! You cannot have your cake and eat it too. In adopting one belief you are rejecting another. Let's be clear about that. It is as true for the agnostic as it is for the Christian.

Secular tolerance is only skin deep. Consider the scientific community's response to Christians who do not believe in evolution. They are ridiculed as obscurantists and reviled as idiotic. It's the Scopes Monkey Trial in reverse! Where, in that famous trial in Tennessee, it was forbidden to teach evolution as a school subject, today it is forbidden to teach creation. Religious dogma is tolerated as long as it does not contradict secular dogma! That's the reality of modern tolerance.

Response

My response to relativism is two-fold:
— It is logically inconsistent
— It is unliveable

First, relativism is logically inconsistent, even self-contradictory. Try this on for size: 'There are no absolutes.' But that very statement is an absolute. Here's another one: 'Everything is relative.' Including that statement itself? If the very statement, 'Everything is relative,' is relatively true then that leaves the door open for absolutes to enter in certain situations. So there are absolutes.

I am not offering up any word-trickery, slipping away with intellectual sleight-of-hand. Our brains can only think in terms of absolutes. Anyone who thinks he is not is only fooling himself. The relativist actually believes in absolutes, just not in Christian absolutes. He uses absolutes, but he keeps them under the table where even he cannot see them.

Secondly, thorough-going relativism is unliveable. While denying the existence of absolutes, your conscientious relativist will be out campaigning for the rights of baby whales and nuked seals as if they really mattered. He will be passionate about cruise missiles or the starving in Ethiopia even while his philosophy is telling him that human life is relatively unimportant (another way of saying relatively important).

When I was in college I had to write a term paper for my philosophy class on 'How do I know I know?'. How did I know that a straight spoon which appeared bent in the water was not really a bent spoon which only appeared straight when put in the deceiving light of the fresh air? In the end, I had no reliable grounds for answering one way or the other. But that didn't mean that I grew uncertain about my spoonmanship. I have never to this day aimed for my mouth and hit my cheek due to a spoon appearing straight but which in reality veered off to the side. Let me clarify: I *have* hit my cheek, but only due to my bad aim. The spoon was straight and innocent.

We may not be sure as to why there are absolutes, but we know there are. We live as if there were absolutes. It's impossible to live any other way. The relativist is forced to live in 'existential hypocrisy'. He believes one thing and lives another. He is like Lincoln Steffens, a Western intellectual who, upon returning from 'Uncle Joe' Stalin's Workers' Paradise in the 1930s, said, 'I am a patriot for Russia; the future is there; Russia will win and save the world. That is my belief. *But I don't want to live there!'* Relativism cannot be lived. No one wants to live there.

If a philosophy is both inconsistent and unliveable I would say that philosophy is probably untrue. Something making sense and fitting reality is as good a test of truth as we are ever likely to get. Relativism fails on both grounds.

Surely you don't believe in Noah's Ark?

'Surely you don't believe in Noah's Ark and all that?'

The only answer to that is, 'Of course I do—and stop calling me Shirley!'

Relativism is the natural consequence of naturalism. Naturalism denies the supernatural and dismisses the Bible's miracle stories as superstitious mumbo-jumbo, a throwback to the Middle Ages. Belief in the supernatural surely reveals a mentality more at home in the primitive ages before the dawn of science. It's backward! Science is glorified. Hard evidence is king.

But in fact hard evidence is not king; naturalist philosophy is king and it will explain away the facts if it has to. Modern, Western man lives under an all-consuming prejudice: a prejudice against the supernatural.

Twentieth-century man knows Noah's Ark is a fable not because he has evidence to the contrary but because 'things like that just don't happen'. He knows Jesus didn't multiply the loaves and fishes not because he has eye-witness reports telling him otherwise but because 'miracles are a hoax. Everything has a natural explanation.'

This prejudice is at work all around us. Veteran political analyst, Gary Wills, once commented on the presidential aspirations of one-time televangelist Pat Robertson, saying, 'The kook factor will do Robertson in.... Reagan believes in miracles...but he never wrestled with a hurricane on television.... Bringing the Holy Ghost in on the cure of haemorrhoids seems, on the face of it, to disqualify the practitioner of such "solutions" from sitting with the National Security Council on more complicated matters.'[57]

Robertson believes in the supernatural so he must be a kook. It is obvious to this political analyst that anyone who believes in faith healing in this day and age may be entrusted with a broom (and even then, if you don't watch them carefully, they may try to climb on it and fly!), but not with much else. Obviously anyone who believes in the supernatural has a less than subtle mind. Anyone displaying such a backward lack of sophistication is not fit for high political office. Obviously! This is prejudice speaking. Wills does not even feel the need to examine Robertson's other credentials. This one fact is enough to disqualify him.

Primitive tribes have a narrow interpretative framework which leads them to conclude that everything has a spiritual explanation: sicknesses are from curses and famines a sign that the demons need appeasing. Modern man exchanges this for a different, yet equally narrow, interpretative framework and says that everything has a natural explanation. It is simply a new prejudice, updated with a bit of chrome and glitz for the twentieth century.

The Christian believes in hard evidence. That is the point of the miracles. But he also believes with Blaise Pascal that 'the heart has reasons which Reason can never know'.[58] Science is not the only avenue of truth. Intuition, conscience, spiritual 'knowing' all have their place.

CS Lewis railed against those who exalted the intellect while debunking sentiment. He said our hearts (our chests) as the seat of our emotions were a vital relay station between our intellects and our animal appetites. He wrote:

> Without the aid of trained emotions the intellect is power-less against the animal organism.... The head rules the belly through the chest....
>
> [narrow scientism] produces what may be called Men without Chests. It is an outrage that they should be commonly spoken of as Intellectuals. This gives them the chance to say that he who attacks them attacks Intelligence. It is not so. They are not distinguished from other men by any unusual skill in finding truth nor any virginal ardour to pursue her. Indeed it would be strange if they were: a persevering devotion to truth, a nice sense of intellectual honour, cannot be long maintained without the aid of a sentiment which Gaius and Titius [whose book Lewis is responding to] could debunk as easily as any other. It is not excess of thought but defect of fertile and generous emotion that marks them out. Their heads are no bigger than the ordinary: it is the atrophy of the chest beneath that makes them seem so.[59]

Science is not the only avenue of truth. Granted, religion like love cannot be measured in a test tube, but that does not mean that its truth claims are second rate. Life was never meant to be squeezed into a test tube. It's too big for that.

Scepticism is overrated

Relativism is the natural outgrowth of scepticism. Rigid scepticism ends up doubting not only faith but even one's ability to know. Intellect doubts itself and, behold, relativism is born!

The sceptical mind-set is much admired in the Western world. Scepticism is taken to be the sign of a sharp mind. Faith is seen as gullibility, as the mark of an unsophisticated simpleton unable to resist the lures of any two-bit, snake-oil salesman who comes by peddling his religious wares.

I say that scepticism is overrated. I say any third-rate philosopher trying to upgrade to second-rate can defiantly say, 'Prove it.' I once heard a man on a radio phone-in programme say that he doubted whether the Americans had ever landed a man on the moon. He thought they had just rigged it all up in a studio. 'You can't put one by me!' he said. Was his scepticism the evidence of a sharp mind or a dulling paranoia? I leave the answer to you.

It is commonly assumed that the scientific mind-set is predominantly one of doubt and scepticism. But this is only part of the picture. Michael Polanyi, physical chemist and Fellow of the Royal Society, writes:

> It seems clear, however, that this method [of radical scepticism and empiricism] does not represent truly the process by which liberal intellectual life was in fact established. It is true that there was a time when the sheer destruction of authority did progressively release new discoveries in every field of inquiry. But none of these discoveries—not even those of science—were based on the experience of our senses aided only by self-evident propositions. Underlying the assent to science and the pursuit of discovery in science is the *belief* in scientific premises to which the adherents and cultivators of science must *unquestionably assent*. The method of disbelieving every proposition which cannot be verified by definitely prescribed operations would destroy all belief in natural science (my emphasis).[60]

Scepticism was never the heart of science; faith in the scientific approach is at the heart of science. Polanyi goes so far as to compare science to religion, saying that both are 'faith in search of understanding'.[61]

The scientific enterprise depends first on faith and only secondly on doubt. Faith is what gives rise to certain hypotheses which scepticism then works on. In this sense scepticism is parasitic on faith. It has nothing to work on until creative faith comes up with an idea.

Faith is what is behind the discovery mode of science, and doubt is behind the proof mode. Both are needed for scientific advancement. W Beveridge, another scientist, likens the interplay between discovery and proof to a courtroom. He writes:

> The methods and functions of discovery and proof in research are as different as are those of a detective and of a judge in a court of law. While playing the part of the detective the investigator follows clues, but having captured the alleged fact, he turns judge and examines the case by means of logically arranged evidence. Both functions are essential but they're different.[62]

The judge is vital, but so is the detective. Without him the judge has no evidence to work with. Without the detective the judge would be retired. He would have nothing to do. Our sceptical faculties are like that. They go to work only after the other faculties—experience, intuition, revelation, etc—have provided the raw material. The problem in the Western world is that these sceptical faculties have thought they could get on without the other faculties. Scepticism reigns. But in reigning it cuts its own throat. Scepticism is exciting as long as there are accepted truths to debunk. Once those are gone it has nothing left to do. Scepticism needs faith to prosper!

Doubt is like a scalpel. If used properly it cuts out unhealthy rot, but if used wildly and indiscriminately it cuts out the very limbs it was meant to help. Use the scalpel, but use it with caution.

The modern world has idolised scepticism, not realising that faith is just as important. Scepticism is not always the partner of the daring and avant-garde. Scepticism can equally be a sign of backward thinking. Beveridge, commenting on the fact that most new scientific discoveries meet initially with scepticism and ridicule, said, 'Scepticism is often an automatic reaction to protect ourselves against a new idea.'[63]

Faith is daring. Faith is willing to step out and believe where everybody else wants to play it safe. Faith, not scepticism, is the engine of human progress. And faith is the gift of God unto salvation. Let's hear a cheer for faith. Don't be ashamed of it and don't allow this world to think that, whistling along comfortably in its 'progressive' scepticism, it has 'outgrown' the need for faith. That's a delusion deadly to the soul. Demolish it and you will be doing the world a favour.

I4

Do It!

Church Growth: America magazine gave the following parable:

Now it came to pass that a group existed who called themselves fishermen. And lo, there were many fish in the waters all around. In fact, the whole area was surrounded by streams and lakes filled with fish. And the fish were hungry.

Week after week, month after month, and year after year these, who called themselves fishermen, met in meetings and talked about their call to go about fishing.

Continually they searched for new and better methods of fishing and for new and better definitions of fishing. They sponsored costly nationwide and worldwide congresses to discuss fishing and to promote fishing and hear about all the ways of fishing, such as the new fishing equipment, fish calls, and whether any new bait was discovered.

These fishermen built large, beautiful buildings called "Fishing Headquarters." The plea was that everyone should be fishermen and every fisherman should fish. One thing they didn't do, however; they didn't fish.

All the fishermen seemed to agree that what is needed is a board which could challenge fishermen to be faithful in fishing. The board was formed by those who had the great vision and courage to speak about fishing, to define fishing, and to promote the idea of fishing in far-away streams and lakes where many other fish of different colours lived.

Large, elaborate, and expensive training centres were built whose purpose was to teach fishermen how to fish. Those who taught had doctorates in fishology. But the teachers did not fish. They only taught fishing.

Some spent much study and travel to learn the history of fishing and to see far-away places where the founding fathers did great fishing in the centuries past. They lauded the faithful fishermen of years before who handed down the idea of fishing.

Many who felt the call to be fishermen responded. They were commissioned and sent to fish. And they went off to foreign lands... to teach fishing.

Now it's true that many of the fishermen sacrificed and put up with all kinds of difficulties. Some lived near the water and bore the smell of dead fish every day. They received the ridicule of some who made fun of their fishermen's clubs. They anguished over those who were not committed enough to attend the weekly meetings to talk about fishing. After all, were they not following the Master who said, "Follow me, and I will make you fishers of men?"[64]

Point made. Don't just learn about evangelism, but do it. A book on evangelism is only useful if we use it to go out and evangelise. We learn by doing in the Christian life. It's fly-by-the-seat-of-your-pants stuff. So do it, and may God bless you in the adventure that will be yours.

APPENDIX

The Gospel and Western Society

The gospel transforms cultures as well as individuals. It not only saves an individual in eternity, it changes a culture in the here and now. My contention is that the West's technological and economic achievements are rooted in the Christian gospel. This gospel's worldview saturated the Western mind through centuries of preaching and teaching. Even those who were not personally committed to Christ picked up the rudiments of this worldview. Soon science was born.[65]

Yes, science needs faith to flourish. As Michael Polanyi, scientist and Fellow of the Royal Society, writes,

The framework of scientific theories contains general theories which cannot be put directly to an experimental test of truth or falsity...no one can become a scientist unless he presumes that the scientific doctrine and method are fundamentally sound and that their ultimate premises can be unquestionably accepted. We have here an instance of the process described epigrammatically by the Christian Church Fathers in the words:...faith in search of understanding.[66]

These 'unquestionably accepted ultimate premises' which enabled science to flourish in the West were supplied by the gospel worldview. CS Lewis writes:

> Professor Whitehead [the famous, if not particularly Christian, Cambridge logician and mathematician] points out that centuries of belief in a God who combined "the personal energy of Jehovah" with "the rationality of a Greek philosopher" first produced that firm expectation of systematic order which rendered possible the birth of modern science. Men became scientific because they expected Law in Nature, and they expected Law in Nature because they believed in a Legislator.[67]

Father Stanley Jaki OSB, the Hungarian born historian of science, wrote *Science and Creation* in which he asked why science should have begun in the West rather than in any of the other advanced civilisations which shone on the world stage. He explains the stillbirth of science in ancient Hindu, Chinese, Mayan, Egyptian, Babylonian, and Greek cultures—all of which could boast a valuable start in science—as rooted in their deficient, pagan worldviews. It was only the Christian worldview dominant in the West ('Christendom') with its faith in progress (versus endlessly repeating cycles of history), its confidence in the rationality of the universe (versus an animistic world wherein events were explained in terms of spirit forces), its affirmation of creation as good (versus the Hindu's rejection of creation as illusion [maya] or the Greeks deriding of practical, manual work as vulgar) which opened the way for the birth of science. He writes, 'Great cultures, where the scientific enterprise came to a standstill, invariably failed to formulate the notion of physical law, or the law of nature. Theirs was a theology with no belief in a personal, rational, absolutely transcendent Lawgiver, or Creator... To this belief science owes its very birth and life.'[68]

Father Jaki refers to J Needham, a leading Western historian of Chinese science, who, as a Marxist, would lean towards an economic explanation rather than a theological explanation of the beginning of science. Yet even Needham admits that

> it is the a-theological orientation of traditional Chinese thought that should ultimately be singled out as the decisive factor which blocked the emergence of a confident attitude toward systematic scientific investigations. All this stood in sharp contrast with the situation prevailing in Western Europe. There, according to Needham's admission, all the early cultivators of science drew courage for their pioneering efforts from their belief in a personal and rational Creator.[69]

What about economic development? Can the economics of the West really have anything to do with the otherworldly gospel? Does the West owe its material prosperity to the gospel? In large part, yes. The biblical principles of diligent labour, frugality, self-help, helping others, honesty and truthfulness will, if applied to our everyday lives, lead to economic betterment.

Max Weber's classic, *The Protestant Ethic and the Spirit of Capitalism*, investigated what motivated modern, thrusting, eager-to-develop capitalism to emerge out of the non-growth, static medieval economy in Europe. His famous answer was: the protestant 'work ethic'; an ethic of hard work, thrift, honesty, rationality and austerity. Weber saw the Reformation carrying the energy of godly virtues out into worldly callings. It was this that led to centuries of sustained economic growth in the West.

Lawrence Harrison, in summing up and quoting Weber, writes:

> He [Weber] believed that at the root of achievement is a set of values and attitudes we associate with the Protestant work ethic: hard work, thrift, honesty, rationality, austerity—in sum, "asceticism." Particularly in the Protestant denominations influenced by Calvinism, they operate in a mutually reinforcing way. The Calvinist concept of "calling"—"the fulfillment of the obligations imposed on the individual by his position in the world"—coupled with the concept of "election"—the belief that God has blessed a chosen few whose state of grace is apparent from their prosperity—"must have been the most powerful conceivable lever for the expansion of that attitude toward life which we have called the spirit of capitalism." And, "when the limitation of consumption is combined with this release of acquisitive activity, the inevitable practical result is obvious: accumulation of capital through ascetic compulsion to save."[70]

The phenomenon called 'redemption and lift' is well-known to church growth analysts. They point out that if working-class converts do not reach out to their peers in the first generation after their conversion they are not likely to reach them in the next generation. Why? Simply because by the next generation the Christians will most likely have risen to a higher economic class and the resultant social barriers will make effective communication less likely. The biblical values of self-restraint, saving for the future, and diligent work results in economic betterment. Converts stop drinking too much, cease gambling away their money, care for their children, become readers (it's difficult to read the Bible otherwise). Social lift follows spiritual redemption.

John Wesley made the same observation two centuries ago when he wrote, 'For religion must necessarily produce both industry and frugality, and these cannot but produce riches.'[71]

Wealth comes from God's blessings, from technological aptitude and from a society in which biblical attitudes hold sway. When the writer of Proverbs wrote, 'Lazy hands make a man poor, but diligent hands bring wealth' (Prov 10:4), he was saying that sustained economic well-being was not primarily a matter of luck but was a matter of human attitude. Where biblical attitudes reign, economic development is sure to come.

Lawrence Harrison, after working for years in Latin America on development problems, wrote a book entitled *Underdevelopment Is A State Of Mind*. He asks why Latin America, which in 1700 was incomparably richer, more powerful and more likely to succeed than the British colonies of North America, today lags so far behind. He finds his answer is cultural attitudes. Contrary to the 'Protestant work ethic', the Spanish mind (the dominant cultural influence in Latin America) saw wealth as something to be obtained through battle and conquest, work was for the slave, commerce for the Jew, fatalism a way of life ('life is shaped by forces beyond human control'). With this mind-set economic development was never going to happen.

If it is true that biblical values lead to prosperity in a culture then it is also true that the abandonment of these values threatens a culture's prosperity. Daniel Bell, Jewish sociologist and Harvard professor, believes that our Western culture is in crisis because of the contradictions between the norms demanded in the economic realm (efficiency, utility, self-sacrifice) and the norms of self-realisation and hedonism now central in our cultural realm. These contradictions are splitting our society apart.

213

Our modern bourgeois culture began in the sixteenth century. Its fragile beginnings were only possible because the cultural norms reinforced the economic norms; discipline, regularity and deferred gratification—norms needed in the marketplace—were reinforced in the cultural sphere by the Puritan ethic enjoining self-restraint and work as a vocation. But we have lost this belief in God and the resultant Protestant work ethic has gone with it. Hedonism and 'self-realisation' is the new ethic.

Bell questions whether our economic performance can be sustained without the cultural root of Christian self-restraint. Furthermore, Bell wonders whether our culture can survive without these roots. From whence comes the dynamic? Quoting Schumpeter, he remarks, 'The stock exchange is a poor substitute for the Holy Grail.'[72]

He writes, 'The real problem of modernity is the problem of belief. To use an unfashionable term, it is a spiritual crisis.'[73] He goes on to say that society needs religion but that religion 'cannot be manufactured'.[74]

What a refreshingly frank admission! Bell is saying that sociologists can analyse the problem, but they cannot provide the solution. They can tell why things went wrong, where things went wrong and when things went wrong.[75] But knowing why one is drowning, where one is drowning and when one is drowning is not nearly so helpful as an oncoming lifeguard. One concrete solution is worth ten expert analyses of the problem.

This is the unique role of the evangelist. He has a message which can transform a culture. He brings God's answer. He can do what no one else can do. Politicians give policies, farmers give bread, but the evangelist gives the bread of life. He has a word from God for a people who have nowhere else to go: 'Lord, to whom shall we go? You have the words of eternal life' (Jn 6:68).

Notes

1. The Galileans were regarded as a slightly backward and untutored part of Israel. They even had their own 'up-country' accent marking them out (see Matthew 26:73). They would have filled the part that in popular mythology the Irish play to the English, the Polish to the American, the Frisians to the Dutch. One knowledgeable commentator on Jewish affairs has written: 'There was a general contempt in Rabbinic circles for all that was Galilean. Although the Judean or Jerusalem dialect was far from pure, the people of Galilee were specially blamed for neglecting the study of their language, charged with errors in grammar, sometimes leading to ridiculous mistakes. "Galilean—Fool!" was so common an expression....' Alfred Edersheim, *The Life and Times of Jesus the Messiah* (Eerdmans: Grand Rapids, Michigan, USA, 1971).

2. Tom Sine, *The Mustard Seed Conspiracy* (MARC Europe: Eastbourne, 1985).

3. C Peter Wagner, *Your Spiritual Gifts* (Regal: Ventura, California, USA, 1983), p 91.

4. Joseph C Aldrich, *Life-Style Evangelism* (Multnomah: Portland, Oregon, USA, 1981), pp 15–16.

5. Catherine Bramwell-Booth, *Catherine Booth* (Hodder & Stoughton: London, 1973), pp 113, 158, 206.

6. A 'freak' is a strange being of the human variety which flourished in the 1960s and 70s but which has now become extinct save for parts of Wales, central Copenhagen, and in the hills of New Zealand/Australia. A 'freak' had three distinguishing characteristics: long hair, belief in the blessedness of marijuana and hashish, and a romantic desire to live in harmony with nature; which desire lasted as long as he stayed out of the state of nature. I speak with complete sympathy for such beings as I was one.

7. *Leadership* (Spring 1985), p 69.

8. James Engel, *Contemporary Christian Communications* (Thomas Nelson: Nashville, Tennessee, USA, 1979), p 81.

9. Hillsborough is the name of the suburb outside San Francisco where I was born and raised.

10. 'Jesus freak' is a highly technical sociological term which was used in the decade of the 1970s to describe hippies who had been converted to Christ but who kept their hippy attire—albeit more cleaned up.

11. Lyle Schaller, *Assimilating New Members* (Abingdon: Nashville, Tennessee, USA, 1982).

12. Charles and Win Arn, *The Master's Plan For Making Disciples* (Church Growth Press: Pasadena, California, USA, 1982), p 43.

13. Win Arn, 'Mass Evangelism: The Bottom Line' in *The Pastor's Church Growth Handbook*, edited by Win Arn (Church Growth Press: Pasadena, California, USA, 1982), vol 1, pp 99–100.

14. Kenneth Scott Latourette, *A History of the Expansion of Christianity* (Zondervan: Grand Rapids, Michigan, USA, 1976), vol 1, pp 116–117.

15. Quoted by Rebecca Manley Pippert in *Out of the Saltshaker: Evangelism as a Way of Life* (Inter-Varsity: Leicester, 1980), pp 66–67.

16. *ibid*, pp 85–86.

17. Phillip Elkins, 'A Pioneer Team in Zambia, Africa' in *Perspectives on the World Christian Movement*, edited by Ralph Winter and Steven Hawthorne (William Carey Library: Pasadena, California, USA, 1982), p 683.

18. Dr and Mrs Howard Taylor, *Biography of James Hudson Taylor* (Hodder & Stoughton: London, 1973), pp 156–159.

19. I should, perhaps, make it clear that I do believe the Bible teaches there are specialist ministries; ministries majoring in one or two gifts which we do not all major in. Each Christian has a specialist ministry; some gifting he is particularly called to. The apostle Paul is talking about specialist ministries in 1 Corinthians 12:28–31 where he writes,

And in the church God has appointed first of all apostles, second prophets, third teachers, then workers of miracles, also those having gifts of healing, those able to help others, those with gifts of administration, and those speaking in different kinds of tongues. Are all apostles? Are all prophets? Are all teachers? Do all work miracles? Do all have gifts of healing? Do all speak in tongues? Do all interpret?

The clear answer to Paul's rhetorical question is, 'No, all do not teach, prophesy, heal, etc.' There are gifts we specialise in. When we find we are especially adept at one gift and when we find we are more apt to be a blessing through that gift than some of the others, then we have found our ministry; our particular area of service (ministry simply meaning service). That's our specialist ministry.

However, while acknowledging the existence of specialist ministries, Paul is not saying that the gifts making up these ministries are exclusively theirs. Prophecy, for instance, is not the exclusive preserve of the prophet. There is a specialist ministry of prophecy, but there is the possibility of 'everybody...prophesying' (1 Cor 14:24). That is why Paul urges the entire Corinthian congregation to prophesy rather than limiting his exhortation to prospective prophets.

Paul was not saying that not everybody could ever heal or teach, he was saying that not everybody majored in healing or teaching. Everybody could at times see these gifts come through their lives, but not everybody had a ministry in these areas. In other words, each of us is a 'Jack-of-all-trades, master of some'.

20. Bill Subritzky, *Receiving the Gifts of the Holy Spirit* (Gift: Costa Mesa, California, USA, 1982), p 27.

21. Quoted in Thomas J Peters and Robert H Waterman, *In Search of Excellence: Lessons From America's Best-run Companies* (Harper & Row: London, 1982).

22. A W Tozer, *Paths to Power* (Marshall, Morgan & Scott: London, 1972), pp 15–16.

23. Subritzky, *op cit*, pp 44–45.

24. Arnold Dallimore, *George Whitefield: The Life and Times of the Great Evangelist of the Eighteenth Century Revival* (Banner of Truth: Edinburgh, 1970), pp 263–264.

25. Percy Livingstone Parker, ed, *The Journal of John Wesley* (Moody Press: Chicago, Illinois, USA), pp 121–124.

26. Quoted in Garth Lean, *Strangely Warmed* (Tyndale: Wheaton, Illinois, USA, 1979), p 122.

27. JC Ryle, *Christian Leaders of the 18th Century* (Banner of Truth: Edinburgh, 1978), p 82.

28. Hubert Lindsey, *Bless Your Dirty Heart* (Logos: Plainfield, New Jersey, USA, 1973), pp 41–42.

29. *ibid*, p 22.

30. *ibid*, p 22.

31. Joe Ellis, *The Church on Purpose* (Standard: Cincinnati, USA, 1982), p 97.

32. John Stott, *Between Two Worlds* (Eerdmans: Grand Rapids, Michigan, USA, 1982), p 137.

33. CH Spurgeon, *Lectures to My Students* (Marshall, Morgan & Scott: London, 1973), p 266.

34. *ibid*, p 349.

35. Catherine Bramwell-Booth, *Echoes and Memories* (Hodder & Stoughton: London, 1977), p 109.

36. Quoted in Stott, *op cit*, p 235.

37. Arnold Dallimore, *George Whitefield*, vol II (Banner of Truth: Edinburgh, 1980).

38. Lindsey, *op cit*, p 17.

39. R and L Lewis, *Inductive Preaching* (Crossway: Westchester, Illinois, USA, 1983), p 137.

40. Ted Engstrom, *Your Gift of Administration: How to Discover and Use it* (MARC: Eastbourne, 1985).

41. D Martyn Lloyd-Jones, *Preaching and Preachers* (Hodder & Stoughton: London, 1976), p 58.

42. John Pollock, *Moody Without Sankey* (Hodder & Stoughton: London, 1966), p 25.

43. Paul Kurtz, editor, *Humanist Manifestos I and II* (Prometheus: Buffalo, New York, USA, 1979), p 4.

44. CS Lewis, *Mere Christianity* (Fontana: London, 1970).

45. John Haley, *Alleged Discrepancies of the Bible* (Baker: Grand Rapids, Michigan, USA, 1977), p 326.

46. Referred to in FF Bruce, *The Spreading Flame* (Paternoster: Exeter, 1982).

47. Quoted in FF Bruce, *The New Testament Documents: Are They Reliable?* (Inter-Varsity: Leicester, 1960).

48. Josh McDowell, *More Evidence That Demands a Verdict* (Campus Crusade for Christ: San Bernardino, USA), pp 309–311.

49. Quoted in Werner Keller, *The Bible As History* (Hodder & Stoughton: London, 1969), pp 179–180.

50. CS Lewis, *The Problem of Pain* (Fount: London, 1977).

51. *ibid.*

52. Victor Frankl, *Man's Search For Meaning* (Hodder & Stoughton: London, 1987).

53. Paul Johnson, *Modern Times* (Harper & Row: New York, USA, 1983), pp 1, 3, 4.

54. Allan Bloom, *The Closing of the American Mind* (Simon & Schuster: New York, USA, 1987), p 25.

55. Quoted in Gerald Coates, *Gerald Quotes* (Kingsway: Eastbourne, 1984), p 49.

56. *The Spectator* (June 14, 1986), pp 10, 12.

57. *Time* (February 22, 1988), p 28.

58. Quoted in Charles Colson, *Kingdoms in Conflict* (Hodder & Stoughton: London, 1988).

59. CS Lewis, *The Abolition of Man* (Fount: London, 1978).

60. Michael Polanyi, *Science, Faith and Society* (University of Chicago Press: Chicago, USA, 1964), p 76.

61. *ibid*, p 45.

62. WIB Beveridge, *The Art of Scientific Discovery* (Vintage: New York, USA), p 123.

63. *ibid*, p 147.

64. Quoted from Charles and Win Arn, *The Master's Plan For Making Disciples*, pp 11–12.

65. Of course, it is true that Christianity has not been the sole contributor to the Western mind-set. Greek philosophy, Roman political thinking and Enlightenment rationalists have all had their say. Nevertheless, it is indisputable that Christianity has played a major role.

66. Polanyi, *op cit*, pp 12, 45.

67. CS Lewis, *Miracles* (Fontana: London, 1960).

68. Stanley L Jaki, *Science and Creation* (Scottish Academic Press: Edinburgh, 1974), p viii.

69. *ibid*, p 40.

70. Lawrence Harrison, *Underdevelopment Is A State Of Mind* (Harvard University Center For International Affairs and Madison Books: Massachusetts, USA, 1985), pp 22, 23.

71. Paul Johnson, *A History of Christianity* (Penguin: Middlesex, 1980).

72. Daniel Bell, *The Cultural Contradictions of Capitalism* (Heinemann: London, 1976), p xxiv.

73. *ibid*, p 28.

74. *ibid*, p 30.

75. It is perhaps interesting to note that Bell's analysis is essentially a rephrasing and development of John Wesley's analysis of the cycle of spiritual and economic growth leading to spiritual and economic decay.

...I do not see how it is possible, in the nature of things, for any renewal of true religion to continue long. For religion must necessarily produce both industry and frugality, and these cannot but produce riches. But as riches increase, so will pride, anger and the love of the world in all its branches.... Is there no way to prevent this—the continual decay of true religion? We ought not to prevent people from being diligent and frugal; we must exhort all Christians to gain all they can, and save all they can: that is, in effect, to grow rich. (As quoted in Paul Johnson, *A History of Christianity*.)

For further information about Youth With A Mission in the United Kingdom, please write to:

Youth With A Mission
13 Highfield Oval, Ambrose Lane, Harpenden,
Hertfordshire AL5 4BX. Tel. 0582 764773.

Knowing God's Will

by Paul Miller

Christians believe that God has revealed his will to men and women down the ages. The Bible is prized as a perfect and fully sufficient record of his dealings with mankind, containing everything we need to know about his will for us in general.

But how do I check out with God my own personal decisions? Is 'sanctified common sense' enough?

What place should I give to the advice of others, and to 'words from the Lord' given in good faith?

How do I know it is God's voice I am hearing, especially when things don't turn out the way I thought he meant them to?

'This is a book that will answer these questions, and many more! I highly recommend it to you.'
—Floyd McClung, Executive Director, International Operations, Youth With A Mission

Paul Miller is the Director of Youth With A Mission in London.

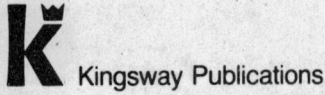

Kingsway Publications